MAKING PEACE
WITH A DANGEROUS GOD

WRESTLING WITH WHAT
WE DON'T UNDERSTAND

LINDA CLARE & KRISTEN JOHNSON INGRAM

Revell
Grand Rapids, Michigan

© 2006 by Linda Clare and Kristen Johnson Ingram

Published by Fleming H. Revell
a division of Baker Publishing Group
P.O. Box 6287, Grand Rapids, MI 49516-6287
www.revellbooks.com

Printed in the United States of America

Library of Congress Cataloging-in-Publication Data
Clare, Linda.
    Making peace with a dangerous God : wrestling with what we don't understand / Linda Clare and Kristen Johnson Ingram.
        p.   cm.
    Includes bibliographical references.
    ISBN 10: 0-8007-3073-9 (pbk.)
    ISBN 978-0-8007-3073-4 (pbk.)
    1. Spiritual life—Christianity. 2. Hidden God. 3. God—Knowableness. I. Ingram, Kristen Johnson. II. Title.
BV4509.5.C515 2006
248.2—dc22   2005033660

Portions of "An Alien God" in part 1 of this book first appeared in *Weavings, A Journal of the Christian Spiritual Life*, in the 2003 issue *Welcoming the Stranger*, vol. XVIII/5.

To our "Sisters in Ink,"

Debbie Hedstrom, Kathy Ruckman,
Heather Kopp, and Melody Carlson.

Contents

Facing the Dangerous God

We tiptoe toward God's heart, trembling.

We find God's presence so irresistible we'd go anywhere he is; at moments this pull toward his love overwhelms us. Other times, God is hard to understand, abrasive, even terrifying. We aren't sure what he wants from us, nor can we say for certain what we want from him. Right now Kris wants a bone marrow donor for her oldest grandson, and Linda pleads with God to help one of her children who's emotionally disturbed.

But what's the final goal? For God to fix what we want, provide us a hiding place, or for us to see God face-to-face?

Rowan Williams, Archbishop of Canterbury, says God "always has to be rediscovered."[1] Which means God always has to be heard or seen where there aren't yet words for him.

Journeying toward discovery of the wild, untamed, dangerous God of the cosmos, we have to jettison some of the popular errors we've learned, the flimsy theology that surrounds us. We hear and see what we don't yet have words for. We write, struggle for the right phrase, pile books on the floors by our desks, leave trails of paper where we walk. The real project is to know God and translate that knowledge into terms we can grab on to.

There's this puzzle, the enigma of God, the uncovering of a hidden Divinity whose laughter warms us and whose majesty knocks us over backward: God is waiting to be rediscovered.

Join us for the trip of a lifetime, a journey to face a dangerous God.

1

THE PUZZLE

Wrestling with the Very Idea of God

Finding the Pieces

KRIS: How many pieces do we have of the puzzle of God?

LINDA: We have Jesus, who has told us everything we know about God. We have the Bible as a road map. We have creation as God's witness, and music and art and amazing food.

KRIS: Everything around us shows us a thumbprint or silhouette or shadow of God; I wish to see a whole picture. So what's the hardest piece of the puzzle for you to find?

LINDA: Why God offers us control and then tells us to let go of it. I'm scared of letting go in my own life, scared to quit managing my family.

KRIS: For the sake of a solution, can you consent to God's management?

LINDA: I don't know. Solution to what? I'm not trying to solve it all, but can't I plan ahead at least?

KRIS: Robert Burns said the best-laid plans of mice and men often go astray. I like the unpredictable.

LINDA: That isn't true. You plan meals. You write first thing every morning. You go to church every Sunday. You just feel surprised by your own routine. I want the safety and calm of knowing what's next.

KRIS: Really? You're really scared when you're not in charge?

LINDA: Yes. But sometimes, I do see the value of what's unforeseen.

Unforeseen and Unexpected

LINDA

Frederick Buechner says if God didn't always arrive unforeseen, we might have all made ourselves scarce long before God got there. I don't know if Buechner means we're too afraid of the light to stick around for God's arrival, but for me it means that when the Lord taps me on the shoulder, God wants nothing less than to control my life.

I'm terrified of relinquishing control. My bent toward managing everything in my life began at a young age, when I underwent several post-polio orthopedic surgeries. In the hospital I focused on my reaction to pain so much that I refused analgesic injections after surgery, fearful of the poke of the needle. I suffered rather than risk a momentary pinprick. I wasn't sure God would rescue me from my ordeal, so I thought I'd have to face it alone. The pain of not knowing what lay ahead was like walking through a dark place in the dead of night.

Over the years I perfected my management style. I went through several more operations, each time terrified that God might abandon me, or worse, that God might let me die. I directed myself never to

cry or act as if I were scared—despite the months away from family and friends and other institutional horrors of the time: hospital
food, hospital clothing, no personal possessions allowed. I looked
as stoic as a patient could be.

Back at home I also worked hard to prepare for any discomfort
I might face. For instance, if I knew I was destined for the dentist's
drill, I'd lie in bed the night before, jabbing my gums with my fin-
gernail, hard as I could. I wanted to simulate the Novocain shot so
I'd know what to expect. If I was ready, in the dentist's chair I could
control my reaction—no squirming, yelling, or crying. I'd be a model
patient because I'd practiced the pain in advance. A lot of the time
I was a wounded animal, ready to pounce. More than anything I
needed to control my world.

I also startled easily. Family members could walk up behind me,
say something ordinary, and then watch me jump and gasp. Hyper-
alertness became my way to avoid unpleasant surprises.

I thought my childhood reasoning worked, in a twisted sort of
way. If I was so afraid of life and of God, then the more I saw what
was coming, the calmer I could be. Except that things, then or now,
rarely unfold the way I think they will.

I'm not a kid anymore, but I still love to control my life. I plan my
day and make detailed lists. My writing time is organized around
a tight schedule involving teaching, editing—and pain control. I
still have to cope with post-polio syndrome, trying to be "energy
efficient" in order to sit upright for a long period. And I still startle
like a kid who's caught raiding the cookie jar.

Over and over the unknown strikes fear into me. I cry out to God
but hear nothing save my own breathing for the longest time. My
need to be in charge drives me to want a firm commitment from
God. "When can I expect you, Lord?" I plead. And it makes me
crazy when God doesn't respond the way I think he should.

I moan that God doesn't care about me. The God who knows everything, who's in control of the universe, feels so far away. Then when I've almost given up, God surprises me, manifesting himself at odd hours. But the God who arrives isn't anything like the God I planned on.

My wishful thinking has imagined a God who should not only find my lost wallet but also be a combination of Santa Claus and my favorite uncle. This no-problem God doesn't annoy me with late-night directives to pray for someone I don't even like. This God never tells me what to do. My idea also includes a God who always agrees with whatever I say, tells me I look fabulous, and writes blank checks for anything I need. Most of all, my fairy-tale God never points out my imperfections and only deals in appearances not substance.

Of course, my imaginary God wouldn't weep with me when awful things happen, because that would be a downer. No problem. Feel-Good God doesn't sympathize with misfortune nor provide me with challenges that build my character. And when I need a helping hand or a miracle to save the day, that God is suddenly on vacation until further notice.

It's a good thing too. When the Ruler of All shows up, imposters disappear. Feel-Good God melts away. The One God, who is light and love, doesn't answer some of my prayers, is always telling me what to do, and bugs me endlessly about things I'd rather not think about, such as offering tougher love to my wayward son. I trot out my phony God to maintain control and for comfort, but the true God, this dangerous Everything, sometimes walks up behind me and startles me right out of the room.

I always need a while to adjust to light. For a time I want to shield my eyes or scurry away to a dark corner like a bug; eventually I stop squinting, throw open the curtain, and see what God is up to. But some days letting go of the reins of my life is so hard.

I haven't wanted to tell anyone about how recently one of my own children took my medication to pay for a drug habit. After all, keeping that information secret from friends who had always given their support might cause me emotional hurt. So I save face—and control. Whether through finances, prayer, or a simple phone call, I know God uses these people to show me love, but I couldn't divulge the awful truth. By admitting my problem I'd make myself vulnerable.

God's surprise in this mess came when I spoke to Kris on the phone. Before I knew it, I'd blurted out my predicament. Her response burst with goodwill, comfort, and prayer. I wasn't prepared to spill my secret, but God provided love and understanding—a perfect answer to my shame and heartbreak.

Lots of times God's surprises upset me because they don't fit with my expectations. God rarely delivers answers like Christmas gifts. And many times that miracle I need so desperately shows up at the last possible second, when I know God could have eased my anxiety sooner. Still, I watch, pray, wait. Sometimes I feign sleep, like a child awaiting Christmas morning, sneaking a peek to see if God's on the way.

I'm not sure why I need to know when or whether to expect the holy. It's not like I'm rushing to clean house or fix a great feast for the occasion. I don't think it's so I can brag that I saw God coming before anyone else. I'm afraid to be surprised by God because I don't want to hand over my life. I'm terrified and yet fascinated by God's love. Real love can never be rehearsed.

Nor can real love be preserved.

The crazy thing about love is that what is true for one situation might change in the next. When my twenty-two-year-old son, whose background is spotted with mental and mood disorders, stole about two hundred dollars from us so he could buy drugs, I grieved. I grieved for my son and his poor choices, almost more than I mourned our own loss. But I didn't think I could give my son harsh consequences and still show I love him.

All day long I yelled at God. I demanded, "Why don't you fix my son?" I raised my face to the sky. "God? Where are you when I need you, anyway?"

But by the next day my love for my son had toughened into a mandate for him: Find a job, repay what was stolen, make a formal apology, go on the antidepressants needed, attend 12-step meetings. I had a whole list of other requirements. I told him all this, knowing I'd have little say in what my son actually decided, but assured him that I would always love him too.

If Kris had hammered me with advice about my son or burdened me with a list of Bible verses to look up, I'd have been put off. But she let me weep into the phone, gave me permission to fall apart, and let me wonder aloud where the Creator could be.

Then God did burst in with a comfort that felt like thick, warm honey.

Why hadn't I seen him coming? How could I have not known?

Deep down I know God is supposed to direct my days. Maybe my problem is God's remedies feel too simple, as easy as a thousand love songs, as real as all the dangers of this world.

Love hurts, because I have to let go.

Love heals when I do.

I'm no less accustomed to letting go than I ever was. Often I still try to soften upcoming blows by practicing control, by prayer or deep breathing. Now and then I poke myself to see what I'm made of; I sleep with one eye open in case God shows up and begs me to take chances, entreats me to make peace with the unforeseen. If I know hours or minutes or seconds before the arrival of the King, I'm not sure I'll be any less prepared for love or any more prepared for danger. All I know is that the unexpected life of love winds straight through the valley of the shadow of death.

The Difficulty of God

LINDA: If control isn't the hardest part of the puzzle for you, what is?

KRIS: I want to understand God. In fact, I want to see God face-to-face. Now.

LINDA: Are you sure? Everyone in the Bible who tried that died.

KRIS: I'm also terrified. What if God doesn't like me? What if I don't like God?

LINDA: Very funny.

KRIS: I'm serious. I've had some glimpses of God I didn't like much, and I don't always see Christ's presence in people who claim they love him. If I could see Jesus Christ in person, then I'd know how he looks in others.

LINDA: What are you talking about?

KRIS: I'm wondering if I would recognize Christ if he were an undocumented Mexican or a Chinese man who came into the country in a cargo box.

LINDA: Well, then, think about him as the Good Shepherd, with the lamb over his shoulders.

KRIS: Oh, sure, and with the long blond hair, straight out of a shampoo ad.

LINDA: (sigh) You're just trying to be difficult.

KRIS: I'm not trying. Life with God is difficult. Let me tell you about the Alien who can make you crazy.

An Alien God

KRIS

I saw the Alien's picture in a recent magazine. He has close-together, intense, black eyes, a prominent nose, rough black hair, and a scruffy beard. If he were standing ahead of me in the airport security line, I'd hope the officials would detain him. I wouldn't want that olive-skinned immigrant on any flight I take.

He doesn't just look sinister. Though he isn't a citizen of this country, he feels free to condemn our culture and our religious practices. He doesn't look like us or act like us, and he is so close to madness he wants us to adopt his ideas. Even when I get on conversational terms with him, I know in my heart that he's destructive to my peace and quiet, that he takes an extremist position about the way I practice my religion, and that he's not only crazy but impractical. As if I could welcome such a man not only into our country but into my private life!

He's anticapitalistic, the enemy of our free market economy and our American business system; he even committed vandalism at an international currency exchange. He believes in some kind of monarchy instead of a democracy, a kingdom with one single, all-powerful ruler. He is already identified as a terrorist. He's a threat to government, trying to recruit Americans to become members of his so-called kingdom. His economic plan is a disaster. He wants to redistribute wealth and invites us to enter intentional poverty, where we'll mingle with thieves, harlots, and homeless street people. And in spite of his insistence that he doesn't own any property, he shows up at some fancy cocktail parties and theaters. His followers have created hundreds of "sleeper" cells right here in America, where they collect vast moneys to fund their cause.

He was sentenced to death in his own country because he threatened the balance of power and the peace of the people, and we in America want to send him back there. Even when we sympathize with his cause for a moment, we don't really like his otherness, his nonconformity, his recalcitrance about adapting to American culture. People have tried to remake him, turn him into a model American, but eventually his strangeness erupts and he scourges our society. The picture I saw, a computer-generated image of him based on anthropological fact, showed up in magazines and disturbed everyone who saw it. The image was too close to the truth, and we turned the page.

So who is this outsider, this scruffy wild man who insists that he, he alone, has the truth about God?

His name is Jesus.

He wants me to sacrifice myself by turning the other cheek, praying for my enemies, forgiving till seventy times seven, donating directly to unworthy beggars, and giving away everything I own so I can follow him.

Who shall abide the day of his coming?

Nobody. So we've created a false messiah and welcomed him into our hearts instead. He is a little like Santa Claus combined with St. Francis. We call on him as Gentle Jesus, meek and mild, or the Good Shepherd, or Dr. Love, who carries lambs on his shoulders and children in his arms and speaks words of comfort to the downtrodden. The kind of savior we like soothes the suffering, comforts the afflicted, and wipes away all our tears.

Of course, Jesus is gentle and kind and a healer, but he's also the Alien who says that self-righteous believers are broods of snakes. He turns tables over in the temple and tells you to cut your right hand off if it wounds your conscience. He suggests that you pay your taxes when you find a magical fish and commands you to forget about the food and clothing and shelter you'll need tomorrow, trusting him to supply it.

We profess to like Jesus, and some secular writers call him a great teacher and psychologist. Great psychologist? If you take him seriously, if you welcome him into your life, you'll find him as abrasive as garnet sandpaper.

Pretend, for the sake of your peace, that Jesus is just one more man, and you've missed a central fact about God: that God is right, and when we disagree, we're wrong. As wrong as Judas or even the devil, as wrong as any sinner who ever existed.

Yet we don't welcome this holy alien. If we brought Jesus into everyday life, we would have no homeless people, no mentally ill men and women wandering in the streets, no kids starved, tortured, or killed in basements. We would quench his thirst by offering water to the people or countries that have none. We might know him as a prisoner when we visit the jails to relieve the inmates' pain and help them find forgiveness and new life. Our attention to the gaps in society would be balanced not by our attention to creating a financially secure future or trying to create a free market economy, but by the amount of time we spend in worship and prayer and service.

The Sermon on the Mount, if it were read to people who hadn't heard it, would probably make them react with horror, just as they did when someone took a copy of the Declaration of Independence to the streets of Manhattan. People thought it was communist propaganda or a terrorist message.

To practice the sermon would be even worse. It would be like standing at the door to Congress, chanting, "Blessed are the peace-makers, for they will be called children of God," while the House debated a nuclear threat from Iraq or Korea or Pakistan. No doubt the sergeant at arms would have you removed. Or it would be like you rising up in a courtroom to shout to the defendant, "If they sue you for your coat, give them your overcoat too." You'd likely get a contempt citation. Or, imagine, if you were to tell the average American male that if he's looked with sexual interest at a woman, he's committed adultery. To make adultery a capital offense would rate raucous ridicule along with bawdy outrage.

I have to face up to Jesus the Alien.

I can't imprison him in gentility or keep him outside the door of my conscience forever. He breaks through walls of stone and appears on either side of locked doors.

Since I can't contain him, I can only give up to him, surrender to him, welcome him. It's disruptive, even terrifying, to become his willing prisoner. Terrible to feel my ambition break and my shoulders relax. Scary to trust someone so unpredictable.

Life without him would be easier.

But what kind of life would that be?

Why Work This Puzzle
When God Seems Absent?

KRIS: I said that life without Christ would be easier, but then I think life without him is no life at all. What do you think?

LINDA: I don't always notice that I have a life with him. Things get in the way. Things like pain and kids in trouble and lame cats. Some days I feel like giving up.

KRIS: Do you think God isn't in your life when trouble strikes? That God is absent when you suffer?

LINDA: Well, if he's present, I'm having a hard time knowing it.

KRIS: It's hard to think and write about Divinity when you're suffering, isn't it?

LINDA: Yes. I'm begging for God's mercy, to stop my distress.

KRIS: Since God didn't stop the Crusades or the Inquisition or the Holocaust, what makes you think you or I will get divine intervention for our misery?

LINDA: Well, even if God doesn't change my afflictions, maybe I'll at least get some peace about them.

KRIS: Don't sell out experience for the sake of peace. Do you ever shake your fist at heaven, Linda? Do you ever call God to account?

LINDA: I think I just want God to share my heartbreak. A big miracle would really scare me. If Jesus showed up, I'd be terrified. So I'm looking for a peaceful heart. Begging for mercy.

Tuesday Peace

LINDA

The winter dark holds off morning as long as it can. I don't want to leave my bed either, to face the day. But I rise and pull on my old bathrobe, one sleeve at a time. I shuffle in slippers toward the coffeepot and feel the weight of everything settle about my shoulders. I offer a silent plea to the Unseen on the way into Tuesday.

My grown sons are at it again. I say this to the Lord, but without making a sound. One son punched a wall and broke his hand the same week he had to find work or risk homelessness. The other son has ongoing substance abuse issues and untreated mental illness.

Why, God? All this and the cat has mysteriously become lame. My own limbs are stiff and sore. There is never enough money.

Of course, God must know this already. But I'm working as hard as I can to help. Does God know I'm heartsick and more codependent than ever?

These family issues aren't new. Shame echoes back at me from the abyss of years of wrangling with lost boys, eking out a living, trying to be more than I am. *Why can't I fix me?* People have given me lots of advice, some of it good and some of it cruel. My back aches with age and muscle weakness from old polio.

In the early dawn I beg God. Peace. Please, a little peace.

I can't say it, but deep down I feel God's dangerously aloof. In my life, peace means the absence of chaos, a respite from guilt and heartbreak. *I want to come home to you, God, but first I need a little break.* The coffee gurgles and drips, not fast enough for my liking. I wait near the kitchen window; watch a gang of crows dive-bomb another bird. The crows call in rasps that sound like *Not enough. Never enough.* Their assault reminds me of the frenzy our family dances, sometimes willingly, most times because none of us can stop.

Maybe I should put my trials in perspective, but like most people, I think my struggles are monumental. I do know if I dwell on problems, they tend to swell to many times their actual size. This doesn't prevent my anxiety. Bloated questions rise above the caws and wing-flaps out in the yard. *Am I ever going to have a normal life? Will I ever feel safe?*

The crows have gone. *Probably not*, I think, though a hint of brightening seeps into the horizon. I strain to hear God's voice, feel around in my heart to see if God has arrived. Faraway, a car backfires. I sip my coffee and try to rejoice in the day the Lord has made.

The cat hops in on three legs and rubs against me.

"Sorry, old boy," I whisper.

He still has an appetite, in spite of his limp. I set his food down and promise to do better by him as soon as I can. He gobbles up his kibble as if he believes I will.

I've heard some people say that to the cat, I'm God. Poor kitty. He thinks he's safe with me.

So this is my crisis on a bleak January morning: Consider whether my God is safe enough to entreat, interested enough to listen, a good enough friend to fall on when I can't stand.

I shiver with cold and with dread in case I don't like the answer. Kitty cleans his face and paws, all the while balancing on his good hind leg. He doesn't look worried.

The coffee wakes me so I can think. Maybe the question isn't, Is God, who's in control, safe? Maybe the question is, Am I safe with God?

To arrive at the conclusion—that terrible things happen in life and there's not much I can do to change it—hurtles me back toward a safe version of God. I go grappling into the morning darkness, scrabbling for the right prayer, the precise words or formula that will guarantee my safety. I plead with the ceiling through unspent tears. *God help me.* What I'm asking is for God to fix all the bobbles and bumbles of my existence. I'm after a God who is as reliable as that old Plymouth I once owned. I want the love of God that goes *with* the grain. I'm as needy as my gimpy cat.

So I plead for peace. Mercy, God. Give my family grace, God. A small loan to tide us over until payday wouldn't hurt.

All around me life goes on its perilous way.

In the midst of the terrible stands this terrible God.

How could I not have seen this before?

A safe God can't fend off evil, can't deliver awesome love. Safety guarantees only limited growth, a narrow view. To tackle life's problems, monumental or trivial, I need this terrible God, the one who's daring and risky, who allows me to grapple with him, feel around in the dark for him.

He's waiting there in the unknown. Solid and terrible.

Maybe there is more safety than I thought in risking everything for a brush with this God who often seems so unknown. To approach the holy, you take a chance. To find out if God really loves, you have to step closer and put your hand in his side. You will feel a hole. Your fingers, your hand will fit there.

The moment I look past my vengeful and distant idea of God to connect with pure Love, misery abates and depression skulks away. I'm no safer than I ever was. Worse, I am powerless.

A pink morning light weaves itself around leafless trees and lands, prismlike on my fingers. A filigree of beauty and possibility spreads before me. I know sunrise won't last long. I hold my breath as the pinks deepen to orange. *If I listen long enough, will I notice that I possess peace?*

The sunrise finally fades into plain Tuesday morning, and I am still grappling, still listening.

I'm headed into it.

The Other Side of the Puzzle

LINDA: I believe in the terrible love of God, but fears of the terrible sometimes get in the way. Aren't you ever afraid of God?

KRIS: Yes, but I'm willing to walk through the dark or the fire to discover what I want. Well, that sounds pretty dramatic. What I mean is my fear of God isn't as strong as my desire to know him.

LINDA: Are you getting closer? Have you received a revelation?

KRIS: Every day with God is another revelation. I think we only catch glimpses of God darkly, as in a mirror.

LINDA: But do you understand how to please God? I'm never sure I make the cut.

KRIS: Oh, man, God is apparently pleased when a snake swallows a rat. I find God trying to please me much of the time, which makes me feel confused.

LINDA: Really? You think God's out to please us? I don't know that it's God's job to please us.

KRIS: Frankly, I don't know what God's job is—if God has a job. I do know God keeps barging into my mind, changing what I think I see into something else.

LINDA: Like what?

KRIS: Let's say my life is a quilt or something. I think it looks pretty awful and then God shows me a different vision . . .

God Is a Patchwork Quilt (and So Am I)

KRIS

My life with God is less like a jigsaw puzzle and more like an unfinished quilt, a swatch of patchwork that's been put away too long so it's rumpled and musty. I lift it out of my mental cedar chest and shake it to see the squares. God's contributions are tidy and colorful, while all of mine are faded or stained, attached with crooked stitches.

I hold that unfinished quilt up to myself, as high as my shoulders, and look in the mirror. The whole is even worse than the parts. The entire object is mismanaged, unplanned. It should be ripped apart and restructured, without any of my own pieces; but then the quilt would be God's alone and if the quilt is my life, the new God-only coverlet would deny my having lived.

What to do? I can tear out the squares and triangles I've added and create better ones, but that too would be denial. To remove my patches would be hiding the facts of my life behind pretty, false stories. So what I have to do is live with the whole and acknowledge that God's ideas are better than mine and that no matter how I try to repair my quilt, my patches will never look like God's.

Still they're mine, after all; the quilt reveals, if not my perfection, at least my memories. One faded scrap of plaid is from a pleated skirt and bolero I wore to first grade, and the wrinkled peach square was left after Nana, my grandmother, sewed me some special pajamas. I wore them in the hospital when I had a mastoid operation. I can't remember exactly what garment the pale blue piece came from, but I feel a quick surge of recognition, a love for what is vaguely familiar. All the patchwork comes not just from outgrown garments but from my life itself.

A beige trapezoid was somehow about the summer when I was forty-one and ran away from home. I run my finger over its soft nap and remember patchouli and hair to my waist and sleeping in the woods. Yes, I had fun that summer. I found out about candles and incense and Sufi dancing, but when I left my family and faith community, I took some people down with me, young students and church friends and one of my nearly grown children. Maybe all of my children.

I put my head back and close my eyes. Odd. The most self-centered times of my life are fragrant and less faded, and the periods when I really did serve my family and the church, when I really was being good, look the most unattractive.

"Fix this," I yell, gazing at the ceiling. I don't know where God lives, but I automatically look upward. Childhood habits die hard. Besides, the author of Genesis did speak of heaven and earth above and below, of vaults and domes and dwelling places. So if heaven is, say, on another continuum that brushes my left elbow, I hope my upward-directed prayer somehow finds its way there. "God!" I call. "Fix my quilt!"

I hold up the quilt, stretching it over my head to display it, so God can see what I mean.

Fix what? God says. I think it's beautiful.

That's God, all right, praising what I think needs a major repair.

So maybe there was no use for those dark, heavy theology texts that I struggled through? Maybe I shouldn't have bothered with meditation and retreats and quiet days? Did I waste my time with prayer and supplication and church? Are all those communions where I took the Body and Blood, which were supposed to exalt my spirit to levels of the Divine, not important to show up in the quilt? How can only the flimsy facts of my life appear, and God think the patchwork is beautiful? How can my quilt or—more plainly—*my self* look beautiful to God, when I've missed the mark so often (and still do)?

One of the things I dislike most is that my life hasn't been so different from anyone else's. My teenage intention to be "different" apparently resonated in all my friends and probably teenagers everywhere, because we were so different from our parents that we all looked alike. Burying my gifts for years is a story thousands of women could tell, and my anger at my mother is a record millions can play. Struggling through menopause and entering old age are awful, but the experience—*drat!*—was not unique to me.

Then what was the use of me? What would the world lose if I dropped dead right now?

A thousand clichés leap into my hearing: Don't talk that way. You're going to outlive us all. If you died, we wouldn't have your books. God isn't through with you yet.

Yeah, yeah. I've heard this all before. I'm rankled that my life is apparently not so matchless as I expected. My service to the world seems so small and piddling. So all my efforts to shine like a star in a crooked and perverse generation haven't been so stellar at all.

Then I hear someone whispering. I'm alone in the house, so I say aloud, "We had our quilt talk. Now run along."

But what about the other one? God says, and spreads out the quilt of his own existence. It's bigger than mine, big as the universe, but it makes me twitchy and uncomfortable. It has too many squares, some of which I recognize and others I never saw before. The outside edge of the quilt looks phony, artificial.

Those are the myths, God says. I can hear laughter in God's voice.

"What's funny?"

People don't understand myths. They think they're false. But some myths come true, like the one about a Savior God who dies and is resurrected. Egyptians, Sumerians, lots of peoples believed in that one.

"Weren't those gods all false?" I ask.

Maybe. Or maybe they were just remembering forward.

"But they couldn't be saved by believing in those gods, could they?"

No one is ever told any story but her own, God says.

I sigh. You sigh a lot when you deal with God. Not the loud stage sigh you may do when your kids act up. This is the one when you know you're beaten but don't feel satisfied. I look at God's quilt again and become more confused than ever. The squares have turned different colors, and I can't find a pattern.

Who is God? What is God? Does God care what I do, or is God only concerned with what I am? Does God ever intervene in human life, or is God *Deus absconditus*—hidden, with a policy of noninterference? Is God passionately involved with my existence? Of all these questions bumping around in my mind, this is the one I utter: "What's the relationship between your quilt and mine?"

I thought you'd never ask, God says. Lookee.

Somehow God's patchwork falls over mine as a transparent overlay. My quilt glows through with celestial hues. Now I can glimpse my whole life as prayer, powerful even while I struggled with relationships and study and work.

Why is God always right? In this light, my quilt is beautiful.

Prayer does it, God says.

"But whose prayers were those?" I ask. "Yours or mine? Does God pray to God?"

Somebody's been praying, God says.

I plead. "Who? Who's been praying?"

That's what this is all about, God says. This searching is to find out. An angel escort comes after God.

I'm left alone. I stand with a spiritual quilt in my hands, hoping God isn't far away.

The Agony of Belief

LINDA: I think God seems the Trickster, like the Native Americans' Coyote. But then I think—no, God isn't a trickster. He's just love, and love is dangerous. So God is dangerous because God is love. The closer I get to love, the more I risk getting not only burned but consumed. I guess we each see this danger from a different perspective. You say you can't get away from God, and I'm always afraid God wants to get away from me.

KRIS: God in my life is like an impish child, shouting, "Let's dance!" when I'm trying my best just to walk. God is too mysterious, too unpredictable. Why should I believe in the God of the Bible? Buddhists have more peace and Hindus more color, while God asks me to believe the improbable scenario of the New Testament.

LINDA: No other world religion claims that God came to earth and walked among us, died to exonerate our collective and individual sins, and then came back to life.

KRIS: What do you think is most dangerous about that belief?

LINDA: If my experiences with non-Christians are any indication, Jesus makes everyone uncomfortable, makes people question themselves, stands us up against a higher standard. Some of the problem is a backlash against politicized Christianity, but the bigger danger appears to be that in-your-face, all-or-nothing, love-your-enemies Jesus. I've got to come to terms with that God, because that God is apparently in pursuit of me. God takes risks and wants me to be free enough to take risks. I want to end my self-consciousness because it keeps me at arm's length from Jesus. And I have to admit that God is irresistible.

KRIS: Hebrews says it's a fearful thing to fall into the hands of the living God, and I'm scared even when those hands are loving. But why isn't living easier? Why so much pain and sorrow? Are you sure God isn't the Trickster?

LINDA: I'm not sure of anything, and God keeps demanding my attention, even when I'm sick or in real physical pain or worried about my kids. And then there's that leap-of-faith thing. Every theologian or philosopher I have read brings it down to that. God does the work but then stands back and waits for you to jump over a river full of alligators and snakes.

KRIS: Maybe we've already made the leap. We can't go back because God is dangerous to ego and stubbornness, a threat to ambition and self-pity. And a loving God is the biggest threat of all. I think Heather Harpham Kopp said it best when she wrote, "Holy, Holy! God is love. Watch out! Watch out!"[2]

2

ASSEMBLING THE PIECES

Wrestling with Proof, Answers, Signs, and Miracles

Wanting the Big Picture

KRIS: I've devoured books on theology and philosophy, but the answer isn't there for me.

LINDA: I'm afraid no amount of reading or discussion can get me into the kingdom, either. I'm still working on that leap of faith.

KRIS: I don't ever remember making a leap of faith. I think people universalize their experience. Aquinas wanted us all to know God through reason, the Reformers said *sola scriptura*,[3] and Kierkegaard was like you, a leap-of-faith man.

LINDA: Okay then, when did you decide to believe?

KRIS: I never did. I was baptized when I was six weeks old, and by the time I could think, I was already a Christian.

LINDA: But doesn't everyone have to make a decision for Christ?

KRIS: I think *you* did. God wanted you to consciously choose Jesus, while he let me just grow up with him. C. S. Lewis said he had to be dragged into the kingdom of heaven, kicking and screaming. Catholics think you have to keep renewing your salvation with good works and the Sacraments, and Baptists believe once saved, always saved.

LINDA: When I was in high school, I used to torment my Christian little sister by talking about all the Chinese babies going to hell because they don't know about Jesus. Who's right? Why isn't God consistent? Why isn't there a rule everyone on earth can understand?

KRIS: There is. Love. That's the law.

LINDA: Then can I have my miracle now?

The Scent of Roses

LINDA

When I was a girl, I longed for a miracle at the foot of my bed. An angel or Jesus might appear at any time—something I both wished for and dreaded. Every night after Mom switched off the lamp, I stared into the dark, hoping, listening, waiting. If a vision had actually appeared, I probably would have died of fright.

A few of my Mexican playmates talked of miracles they'd witnessed. They'd heard angels singing, smelled roses, seen the Virgin Mary weep. My family, staunchly Protestant, said I shouldn't be looking for God in things I could see.

But I wanted—no, had to have—proof of my own. I needed to see an angel in a vision, or Jesus holding out nail-scarred hands—I'd even settle for the Velveteen Rabbit's coming alive if the angels and Jesus were busy. And what about healing? Jesus could fix my paralyzed arm just like he did for that man in the Bible.

"Just one little miracle would be great," I'd whisper to God, "and I'll never stop believing in you, cross my heart and hope to die." Then I'd lie still, barely breathing and watch. I snapped upright in bed at every rustle of wind. I sniffed the air for the telltale scent of roses. Night after night I squinted into the shadows until my eyelids drooped and I fell asleep.

How could I know if God was really there, and if God was, how could I hope to prove it? And why was God invisible, anyway? Maybe God would be easier to find if he wasn't so hard to see.

My grandmother, a devout Southern Baptist, chuckled when I first asked her those questions. She assured me that God was real because of Jesus, who died for me and rose from the dead. "You just keep on believing," she said, a twinkle in her pale blue eyes. "The Lord always reveals himself to those who believe on him."

I wondered if God performed miracles only for certain people, mostly the ones who ate fish on Fridays and kept religious statues around.

My friend Skeeter Martinez and I hung around together after school, climbing on my swing set, spinning ourselves dizzy in the hot Arizona sun. One day we were daring each other to twirl faster, winding the swing chains tighter and tighter, then screeching with delight as we let go. After multiple spins we staggered around the yard in circles, dizzy and goofy. We both sat cross-legged on the lawn.

Skeeter leaned forward and got a very serious look on her face. "My grandma saw the Virgin weep," she said. Skeeter herself had smelled invisible flowers that her grandmother identified as roses.

"How did you know they were roses?" I plucked a long piece of grass, weaving it into a ring. Skeeter's confession intrigued me.

She sniffed. "I just know, that's all." She looked away. "Besides, *mi abuela* says so."

"So that proves it? Your grandmother says so?" My face felt hot and I knew I was stepping dangerously close to a fight with my friend.

But Skeeter didn't get defensive. Her eyes said she felt sorry for me and she sighed. "You don't understand, *gringa*."

Truth was, I didn't understand, but I wanted to, so much that I kept my nightly vigil for years to come. My own grandmother said I didn't need to witness a vision or see a statue weep, unlike Skeeter's *abuela*. Which grandmother was right?

I still don't know. My perception of God is, in some ways, as mysterious and fuzzy now as it was when Skeeter and I played on the swing set. What do I know about God's nature? Along with centuries of Christian theologians, I go in search of answers about who God is and whether or not God is anything like the attributes I usually assign to the Creator. And if I get lucky enough to see some part of God, will I be too scared to look?

The Bible gives me the most help. Scripture says God is love, God is light, God is the Alpha and the Omega. Whew, so far this God doesn't seem too awful. Then I read that God was angry and wiped out whole populations of folks who wouldn't do God's will. Now I'm shaking. Pleasing God wasn't easy for the Israelites, and some days I think God is kind of crabby with me too. If that aspect of God had appeared at the foot of my bed when I was a kid, I think I might've hidden under the sheets.

The Bible also says that the same God who is love also is awesome—and not just really cool as we use the term in slang. No, an awesome God is a God to be feared. Frederick Buechner writes that God "is awful in his majesty and power as he says, 'Let there be light.' He is more awful still as he says, 'I'm lonely—I'll make me a world.'"[4] Awful and stunning, God could scare the life out of anyone who saw him face-to-face.

Prophets who came into contact with God were blinded by awe, so terrified that they had to fall down. Any real vision would put me not only under the bed but crying for mommy. The hair on my neck prickles at the thought of the living God paying me a midnight visit.

What about other sources for knowing God is really there? I perceive God as a feeling—although Grandmother said I shouldn't trust feelings too much. When God bursts onto the scene, I'm never in doubt about God's existence. Some call it a nudge of the spirit. In my church the ringing of bells signifies God's arrival, and my whole body verifies this truth when I hear them. Whether it's a serendipitous chance to help someone in need or being paroled from a punishment I know I deserve, God's arrival is always sudden yet unmistakable. I don't exactly smell roses, but the feeling is unlike any other.

And if God is suddenly absent from me, the feeling is always the same too—an emptiness that goes on forever, the blackest hole, with the crushing gravity that snuffs out light. The few times I've either turned away from God, or worse, had God mad at me, were excruciating. After only moments of feeling cut off from God, I'm crawling back, begging God to speak to me, rabid for the chance to reenter God's presence again.

By the time God shows up again, whether it's been minutes or days, I'm usually ready. And when I ask, "Where were you, God?" the answer's always the same: You're the one who moved. And if I question whether God is really there at all, I end up saying, like good old Skeeter, that I just know, that's all.

If God granted my wish, how much would it cost me? A genuine apparition of Christ, however thrilling, could burn me alive. Buechner calls God the beloved enemy because, "before giving us everything, he demands of us everything; before giving us life, he demands our lives—our selves, our wills, our treasure."[5] The miracle I've been straining to see would change me forever.

My life could never be the same. Even a momentary glimpse would refocus my life on the things that matter. Never would I be able to turn away from someone in need or remain neutral to suffering. Seeing Jesus would surely kill off my inclinations to minimize or deny my shortcomings. Most of all, I could no longer procrastinate about showing Jesus's love to those in my world.

If God let me in on something extraordinary, a true vision would be impossible to control. I'd squeeze shut my eyes, but it would still be there. The miracle I begged for would follow me everywhere, even as I fled in terror. I'd cover my eyes, and the image would be constant—terrible and gorgeous and impossible to resist. I'd peek through my fingers, drawn to my awful enemy, whose name is Love.

In spite of my fear, I long to see God. Every night I gaze into the heavens, whispering that the coast is clear. "You can come out now, God," I say and stare right through Orion's belt. Even though I tremble with awe and dread, I wait. And though a bedtime miracle sounds like a cure-all for an imperfect life or a paralytic arm, I get the feeling it wouldn't be enough. I don't think I could ever get enough of God.

Maybe my Mexican friends like Skeeter and her grandmother knew a similar hunger, one they satisfied through tears on a statue. My own grandmother clung to the faith she knew—one that didn't include apparitions but overflowed with God's love just the same. My childhood wish, while probably based in curiosity or the need to belong, keeps me searching for God no matter what the cost.

I still lie awake at night, aching for that miracle vision. I draw in deep gulps of air, hoping to catch the faint scent of roses, all the while trembling at the possibility of seeing God.

Seeing with Your Ears

LINDA: Until I see God face to face, my dialogue with him has to come through prayer.

KRIS: Do you ever think of prayer as a burden?

LINDA: Sometimes when I pray for other people, I feel responsible for them. If I pray for someone to get a job, I feel as if I need one. Maybe the hard part is knowing whether you're bearing someone's burdens or being codependent.

KRIS: I think codependent means not only praying but managing the situation. My problem in childhood was that I thought if I didn't pray to my Guardian every morning and then for the miners in my town and for my family, we might all die in an explosion or something.

LINDA: That kind of prayer sounds like a talisman, to ward off evil, but a child's view of God is often innocent and trusting.

KRIS: And I felt that burden the most when I wasn't quite six. There was a cave-in at the copper mine.

Palo Verde Prayers

KRIS

Shadows of tall cactus fell on our backyard in the early morning, while quails and mourning doves echoed my waking prayer to my Guardian Angel. Then I prayed for the miners who, a little farther up the hill, flirted daily with death and were already nearly a mile down in the earth. I had to pray so much in a day that I sometimes wished God didn't exist. But if I forgot my morning prayer for the miners, they might be killed in cave-ins or boulders that fell or by falling down the vertical shafts where the cage, or mine elevator, operated. Their lives were my burden or part of it, anyway.

I also prayed about cactus wrens. They nested on top the saguaro cactus and fledged just as the big white blossoms opened, and I was terrified that if they hatched late, they would be either smothered by the petals or pushed out of the nest before they were ready. Then they would fall to the ground, where snakes would swallow them. I asked my parents and my first grade teacher over and over how the wrens, or how the cactus, knew what the days were and how many had gone by.

I asked, "But what if one bird was very little and couldn't fly yet; would it fall out when the flowers opened?" I worried about this at night and during mealtimes, fearful that the flowers would come too soon or the birds leave too late, so that in late spring I could neither eat nor sleep.

One May morning when I was five years and four months old, I was standing on a hill above the mine entrance, watching what looked much like a nest on one tall cactus, praying for the birdlings and praying that someone besides me would pray, when the whistle at the mine below me began to blow repeatedly, its shrill voice binding the town. I ran downhill until I came to where the crowds of women had come up the hill and stood still, pushing their hair back and wiping lard and flour off their hands onto their aprons or skirts. They had herded directly to the entrance of the "cage," an open elevator that operated like a funicular, one car plunging to the deepest shaft openings, while its twin shot upward. A load was coming up now, a load of men whose faces were covered with red and blue rock dust; they were coughing, all except for the one who lay on the cage floor, not moving.

"Move aside, please," shouted one of the two doctors owned by the mine.

"You're too late, Doc," a man on the outside of the cage sobbed; he was holding onto the steel bars as the cage came up and stopped, and he nodded toward the man who lay at his feet. "Dick McGrew died on the way up from forty-eight hundred."

A woman at the back of the crowd screamed and fell back into the arms of those around her. She had bobbed auburn hair, waved at the sides and turned up into a roll at the neck. I watched her tear at the neck of her dress until the voile collar was ruined.

"Anyone else?" someone called.

"Three Mexicans are still under the cave-in, that I know of," said the man from the cage, now out on the ground with his dust-covered companions and heading into the frightened squad of bosses bearing down on him for news. The Mexican women hadn't come to the mine; they stood near the grocery store on the east side of Queen Creek. Like the white women, they did not speak among themselves but waited for some news, some sign. Now someone would have to cross the creek and tell them and listen to their screams too.

Mrs. McGrew began to shout, "O, God, I loved him so, I loved him so." And then my own mother appeared at the back of the crowd, with Julia, our housekeeper, beside her; she called out in her high, soft voice, "Frank Johnson?" and several of the women turned to stare at her.

I stared also. My father was an engineer, who wore a white shirt and a tie to work. Why was Mother looking for him among the miners?

"He was going down to forty-eight hundred to see whether they could drill a new shaft," Mother pleaded, and the crowd parted to let her and Julia through. "Frank Johnson?" she called to men who were emerging from the cages. Some were bleeding. I could see one man's torn ear through a copper-edged grommet in the canvas cage wall. My mother's neck bent forward with anxiety, her wavy hair rippling against her chin as she asked each groaning mass of men who emerged, "Frank Johnson? He was on forty-eight hundred?" And I started to scream.

Probably because Mother could not take her eyes away from the mine entrance, it was Julia who darted across the tracks and picked me up and murmured over and over to me in Spanish as she carried me, still screaming. Mother tried to speak to me, but her lips were lame except for my father's name and geography; she finally gestured toward our house.

"No!" I screamed. "Daddy! I want to wait for him."

Mother had still not taken her eyes away from the cage; as another load of men came up, she stepped forward, my father's name on her lips. This time her incantation made him appear, with his left arm around the neck of another man, and as he hopped, his face contorted with great pain, and his mouth twisted with nausea.

I tore loose from Julia's grasp and pushed through the crowd until I could throw my arms around my father's waist. His cold steel belt buckle pressed into the flesh of my cheek.

"It's all right," he said, reeling for balance against his friend but touching the crown of my hair with his free hand. "I have a hurt leg, but I'm all right."

By now Mother had worked her way up to the front, breathing, "Frank-Frank-Frank," beckoning for the doctor and a stretcher.

"You can't go in the hospital," Mother told me. "Julia will take you home, Kristen. You wait there."

"But Daddy," I said. By now the two men had wrestled my father onto the stretcher and they were bearing him away like fire ants with a leaf between them. I lay down on the ground, sobbing.

"Kristen," Mother said, looking over her shoulder as they bore my father away on the stretcher. With obvious regret for my agony, she said quickly, "He'll be all right, honey," and then she ran after him, light-footed and almost transparent in her organza dress.

I wept for another few moments, defeated, then I pushed myself up with my hands so that small rocks bit into my palms; and I began to walk home, deliberately scuffing the toes of my brown oxfords in the road. Julia cantered down the road behind me, her long brown limbs moving like tree branches in the wind, and she caught up with me at the point where the road turned and the top of Magma Avenue began. My tears merged with the dirt on my face and sent muddy brown streaks onto the front of my yellow cotton shirt. Finally, I took a deep, uneven breath, looked up at Julia and, still crying, said, "*Yo temero mi padre es muerte.* I fear that my father has died in that hospital."

"No." Julia shook her head vigorously, but she also took my hand and said in Spanish, using the familiar "thee" to address me because I was a child, "I believe thy father's leg bone has a breach in it. That can be repaired. He will wear a casting of white plaster for some weeks, and then he will be well. Perhaps he will use a crutch for a brief time but not for always. We will pray," she said as we went through the gate. We stopped in the yard and said the Lord's Prayer in Spanish. After she went inside, I said it again in English, to make sure God heard it. Julia was Catholic, and I wasn't sure about Catholic prayers. That day, I wasn't sure about any prayers; hadn't I prayed for the miners that very morning? And hadn't some got killed anyway?

I waited with my dog, Windy, on the big front porch for my mother to come home from the hospital. I watched for her shoes, dark gray, pointed, T-strap shoes, to dance down the street; I watched for the wind to blow the skirt of her dress, a dress with a rounded neck and no sleeves, the fabric a blurred garden of green and yellow flowers and leaves, with a pale green satin slip showing underneath. And most intently of all, I watched for the flag of my mother's wavy hair, tossing in the wind around her delicate oval face.

After the smelter smoke streamed out at six o'clock, the south of town glowed red with the slag poured onto a great pile of gray rock; they poured the smelted copper into forms for cooling, and the refuse became manufactured lava. Julia lifted me and carried me to the table and sat me in a chair; Windy, my Boston bull terrier, sighed and lay down under the table. By then I had stared up the street until my eyes felt scraped and I was almost asleep. I picked up my lamb chop with grimy hands, and sucked and bit at it until it was clean to the bone, and then I drank my Ovaltine and went into the bathroom.

Julia had boiled a kettle of water and poured it steaming and dangerous into the bathtub. It took four zinc-colored kettles of gurgling hot water for my bath; only the fourth one was really hot, the rest having settled in the tub into various cooler temperatures. Then Julia splashed what was in the tub into the crook of her elbow, to test it; and she pulled my clothes off and heaved me gently into the tub.

"The mother has stayed at the hospital for many hours," I said in Spanish, staring at the gray rubber bathtub stopper. "Dost thou fear for my father?"

"No!" Julia clapped her hands in the water so that it spouted up between them, splashing my chest and chin and making me laugh for a moment. "Thy father will recover, and *Señora* will come home soon to tell thee of his misadventure." She lathered my small body vigorously with Ivory soap, let the bar float while she rinsed me off with the washcloth, then wrapped me in a white towel and lifted me out. Because the water was hard in Superior, the towel was rough-textured and stiff against my skin.

Dried and clothed in pajamas, I sat upright in my bed for a long time, thinking about the deaths of Ralph McGrew's father and the three Mexican men, one of whom was the father of Philip Guzman, a boy in my class. I wondered if Mrs. McGrew would take her son, Ralph, and her tiny baby daughter and move away, or if she would stay in the yellow wooden house, looking around at his sweater still hanging over a dining room chair, and mutter tearfully, "I loved him so, I loved him so . . ." Then I said all the prayers I could remember, including "Now I lay me down to sleep," "Gentle Jesus meek and mild," and the Lord's Prayer, and added the list of people I wanted God to bless.

I had come to believe that after I invoked blessings, God could not smite with death or diseases these persons—my parents and grandparents and aunts and uncles and cousins. As long as I remembered to pray blessings for them nightly and sign off in the name of the Trinity, I was safe. I feared that if I forgot to pray for my grandparents or left cousins out of my blessings, God might send them vile illness or storms that tore the roofs from their houses, or touch them with eternal damnation that ended in a place of fire and devils. I believed this praying to be too great a responsibility for me and often I longed to ask my mother for help in blessing our extended family, but I didn't, because Mother was not articulate about religious things.

I prayed for my father's injuries and begged God not to let him die because I suspected that the thread of my own life was attached somehow to his physical body and that if Frank Johnson were to die, I might also expire, simply curling up like a brown tendril on a sun-devoured gourd vine.

But then I heard my mother's voice, and then my father's, spoken as they got out of the doctor's car and came up through the front gate and onto the porch, with much clumping from Father's cast; and they came into the house. I threw back the covers, so I could run out and leap on my father and thank my mother for bringing him back; but before I could even set my foot onto the floor, I fell into a deep, relieved sleep. Much later, Mother said, she found me that way, flung sideways across the bed with my foot over the edge.

Six weeks after Daddy was injured in the cave-in, Mrs. McGrew packed up to move to her parents' home in Tucson. The mine presented her with a five-hundred-dollar check to compensate for her husband's death; but a clerk from that office, who could not bear unbalanced or incomplete ledgers, sent her a bill for seventy-five cents, for heavy canvas gloves her husband had bought the morning he was killed. Mrs. McGrew tore the bill into strips and took them to the mine office and tried to force John Gardner, the assistant general manager, to eat them. The help of the entire office staff was required to pry her hands from his jaws.

On that same day the doctor removed the cast from my father's leg, and I was relieved of at least a moment of my burden; I no longer had to pray about it. His leg had been set without much skill and Father had not quite a limp, actually more of an idiosyncratic stride, for the rest of his life. He took to standing with his weight on his left leg, his right thumb hooked into his belt, and a look of great mercy on his face.

Prayers of Burden

KRIS: When did you start praying for other people? And did you say, "God bless Mama and Uncle Jerry"?

LINDA: At my house, we prayed, "Now I lay me down to sleep . . . ," but I didn't add the "God bless" parts until I was nine, turning ten, and away from my family for the first time. Then I felt that I had to protect them from anything bad that might happen. My family couldn't protect themselves, and it was up to me.

KRIS: So you had a burden too. I wonder how many people feel that way.

LINDA: And in the hospital ward where I had several orthopedic surgeries, I had to protect the other girls, especially Beatrice, who was crippled by cerebral palsy. Not only did I have to pray for them, but I had to be the answer to my own prayers. I was the only one on the ward who could walk unassisted.

KRIS: How did you do that?

LINDA: I waited on them, carried their bedpans, held basins while they threw up. And I stole Jesus for Beatrice.

Stolen Savior

LINDA

I'd never been away from home before. I was nine years old and having surgery on my polio arm in a hospital for crippled children. It was winter and only the second time I'd seen snow. In Yuma, Arizona, where I was from, snow didn't come except on TV shows. With TV snow, people got lost in blizzards. I said I'd rather have six more surgeries than be lost in a blizzard. On Christmas Eve, 1961, the sky looked like dove feathers. Snow floated down in fat lumpy flakes.

I'd been a patient on the girls' ward since before Halloween. The doctors were waiting to see if their operation on my bad elbow had done any good. While I waited, the eleven other girls and I wrote letters to our folks. We girls learned how to make hot pads, went to Girl Scouts, attended school. Nobody got to skip school unless they had just had an operation and were still throwing up.

Christmas should be a time of peace and joy—I knew this from singing all the songs. Peace and joy, joy and peace. We had to go to church on the ward sunporch, whether we wanted to or not, with awful Nurse Jensen. She had narrow eyes and bumpy cheeks full of craters. She sighed a lot, especially when she had to do church. She was sighing loud that night.

A plaster Baby Jesus, lying very still in a crèche on the activity table, was born to save us from our sins, she said. We weren't allowed to touch him. "He's made of plaster," she said. "You wouldn't want to accidentally break Baby Jesus into a million pieces, now would you?"

I peered at the little statue, which could fit in my hand. I asked, "Is the plaster the same as the stuff we get for our casts?"

"Just don't touch," Nurse Jensen said. "Let's sing." She set the record player needle on a 45, but it wasn't Elvis or "I'll Be Home For Christmas." A lady on the record sang Sunday school songs like someone frying bacon. Sssssss. "Sing," Nurse Jensen repeated. We got the idea we should sing whether we wanted to or not.

The other girls and I launched into "Jesus Loves the Little Children." I knew he loved us red and yellow, black and white, but I was never sure why brown was left off the list. "What about Beatrice?" I'd say. I held up Beatrice's hand. Every night she prayed in Spanish, her chocolate-colored hands clasped together the best she could. This wasn't all that easy for her because she had cerebral palsy. Her fingers usually got tangled like an old necklace.

Nurse Jensen sighed and put on another record. This record crackled and skipped, but we sang "Jingle Bells" loud as we could. We sang the funny version: "Jingle bells, Batman smells, Rudolph laid an egg." Nurse Jensen scowled at me because I started it, but what could she do to me on Christmas?

Some of the nurses tried to cheer us up. They decorated a Christmas tree. It stood in one corner of the porch, crowded with clumps of tinsel and too many ornaments. The branches drooped. Our Christmas tree looked as crippled as the patients.

The tree and I were the only things able to stand up around here, if you didn't count the nurses. Besides being the only lucky kid who could walk around the ward, I was the only one who had brought a Bible. I kept it under my pillow. Beatrice prayed all the time, but she didn't have a Bible. How did she expect God to protect her?

While Jensen went on about cleansing us of our sins, I traced the gold-stamped letters on the front of my King James Version with my fingers. Then Nurse Jensen asked me what sins I wanted to confess to God.

The first thing I thought of was how I'd hidden brussels sprouts from dinner the night before in the drawer of my bedside table. Sharon and Beatrice slipped me theirs too. I wrapped them all in a napkin, smelled them all night long.

Jensen repeated her question. What sins would I lay at the feet of Jesus? I looked over at Baby Jesus, but he didn't move. She sighed again and checked her wristwatch—the same watch she stared at when she took our pulses, three times a day. Sometimes she didn't even write the number down. Nurse Jensen didn't give a hoot whether any of our hearts were still beating.

After a minute I decided she wasn't really interested in how clean my spirit was, either. I lied. "Today I called Sharon a dumb bunny," I said. Right after church I flushed the sprouts. If God wanted the truth, he'd have to ask me himself.

After lights out, none of us could sleep. We whispered about Santa Claus and told about how our families back home celebrated Christmas. Beatrice said her mother and aunts and sisters all went to midnight mass. Other girls said they set out plates of milk and cookies for Santa and his reindeer.

I didn't believe in the Santa stuff, but I kept my opinion to myself. The brussels sprouts were enough trouble for one day. I fell asleep remembering how my father decorated last year's Christmas tree: his air-only whistle as he lay each piece of tinsel perfectly straight, with the angel winking on top.

Christmas morning in the hospital, we girls did all the usual things plus a few special chores. We had to dust and tidy up our nightstands and hide the bedpans and throw-up basins. I helped the girls who couldn't do stuff for themselves. As usual, we made our beds the hospital way: pale green bedspreads tucked in hard all around, the top folded back. We weren't supposed to get the bedspreads wrinkled.

I didn't care if my bed got messed up or not. In fact, I was so excited that I thought I'd explode, because someone said we would get to see a parade. I wondered how we'd stay warm when we went outside to watch. Most of the girls had plaster casts on their legs and couldn't wear shoes. Maybe they could go in their socks.

I thought about all the presents I'd asked my folks to get me for Christmas this year: a complete set of Mark Twain books and maybe a couple of Nancy Drew mysteries, a typewriter to write my own stories, a microscope, and even though I never played with dolls, I asked for a Madame Alexander collector's doll—one from some exotic country like India or France would suit me fine.

At eleven in the morning the head nurse arrived. She ordered everyone onto their beds and shook her head no when someone asked if we were going out for the parade. The beds were nowhere near the windows and we were three stories up. I got the idea we weren't going to see much. We sat on our beds while fa-la-la-la-las drifted with the snowflakes.

When the coast was clear, I sneaked off my bed and went to the window. Down on the street a bunch of red-suited St. Nicks looked up and waved while clowns rode tricycles in circles. The marching Santas yelled, "Merry Christmas!" From where I stood, they looked six inches tall. I wondered why they didn't come inside the hospital.

"Back on your bed," the nurse warned me again. At home Daddy always made my little sister and me wash our faces and brush our teeth before we were allowed to see what Santa had brought. By this time, I thought, my sister had torn through all the wrapping paper, squealed over all the toys. She'd probably already wrecked the hairdo on her new Barbie doll or spilled hot chocolate on her good pajamas. Mother would be cooking and Daddy would be staring at his perfect Christmas tree icicles. After a while I got on my bed like the other girls. We waited for Santa to enter the ward.

Just before lunch a group of grown-ups showed up. Santa carried a big red sack. His beard was angel's hair, soft and shiny. He wore a real velvet suit and too much aftershave and motorcycle boots just like Daddy's. He wasn't Daddy, but the Santa was trying. His ho-ho-hos could have used some work. The other girls oohed and aahed as Santa Claus stopped at each bed.

Motorcycle Santa passed out two wrapped gifts to every girl. We all got excited—they allowed our mommies and daddies to send us presents! I thought about gifts I asked for in my letters home and in a letter to the North Pole that we all had to write for penmanship practice. My heart pounded faster.

We opened our gifts. Beatrice couldn't rip the paper from hers, so I helped her. She got a Japanese doll and a box of pink stationery with a ballpoint pen. These weren't presents from our parents; they were boxes labeled, "For a girl." And didn't they know Beatrice was too crippled to hold a pen?

I rushed back to my own packages and tore the wrapping paper away. The first box held a small doll, dressed in pale blue lace. Rochelle the Southern Belle, the tag said. She was not from India or France—I shoved her aside. The other box held a stuffed reindeer, a ten-inch Rudolph wearing a cartoon smile. My lower lip trembled. I scooped up my gifts and Beatrice's stationery set and I ran.

My feet slapped against the linoleum as I made my way to the entrance of the ward. Wait, Santa. Someone made a big mistake and I was the only girl who could run after him. The head nurse grabbed my shoulders, marched me back toward my bed. Motorcycle Santa and his helpers stuffed themselves into the elevator. The doors whooshed shut.

Maybe the nurses and the doctors were only trying to help. They must have known Christmas was awful if you were stuck in a hospital. We got turkey and trimmings for supper but nobody ate much. All evening long Beatrice whimpered in Spanish; tears dripped off her chin. The nurses couldn't figure out what was wrong.

After lights out I crawled over my bed rails and tiptoed out to the sunporch, where Baby Jesus still lay with his arms outstretched. I knew it was dangerous to touch, but I lifted him from his manger, gently cradling him in my palm. I knew he was only plaster, but somehow I didn't feel so alone.

The snow kept coming and the world was quiet. Rochelle the Southern Belle and Rudolph stared back at me from my nightstand. I squeezed Jesus, but Beatrice still looked sad. I curled her fingers around the painted baby and climbed back into my bed. She fell asleep clutching the Savior, but his arms reached out to me.

The Hunger for Proof

KRIS: Are you still stealing Jesus?

LINDA: I'm not the type to stand on the street corner, preaching and handing out tracts. But I do want to bring Jesus to the world. I don't want to be ashamed of my faith.

KRIS: But are you still stealing Jesus? When you started going to church with me, did you feel like a thief?

LINDA: At first I felt as if I had no right to be there. Someone would find out I was a phony. I didn't even know the words to the songs. But there were aspects of this church that spoke to me directly.

KRIS: Well, you were hoping to smell roses. I want a whole garden.

LINDA: My roses are invisible. How about your garden? Is it a real place?

KRIS: That's what I'm trying to figure out. I'm looking for Eden.

LINDA: Look in the Bible.

KRIS: No, I want the Garden to be real. Like God. I think I want a sign.

LINDA: Like an angel or the scent of roses. I said I still lie awake at night aching for a vision. So are we questioning the existence of God or the proof of Scripture, or are we just hungry for something tangible?

KRIS: Hoo boy. Any answer I can give could come out as heresy. But the Garden is more than just tangible. It's where I want to live, if I find it.

LINDA: Find it? Or be it?

KRIS: Okay, let's head for the Garden.

Journey to Eden

KRIS

Here is my question: Where is the Garden? I want to find the real one, the original. I look at maps and decide Eden was in Egypt or between the Black and Caspian seas, but I haven't heard any archaeologists say, "We found the Garden of Eden. There was an angel guarding the gate with a twirling sword."

According to rabbinical tradition, Jerusalem is the site of the real Eden, at least for the heart and mind of Jews, where the rivers flowing out are the people who take God to the world. Well, I don't want a metaphorical Eden. I want there to be, or at least to have been, some kind of a real place. If not an Eden where the Tree of Life grew in the middle, at least a place where It All Started, the square on the game board where you put your token and rolled the dice. A place from which we were ultimately barred, where we picked the fig leaves for aprons, near where one of God's own precious animals lost its life so we could have clothing.

I want to find some final truth in the Garden, maybe some justification for the fact that once a year my denomination regularly reads from the lectern the account of Adam, Eve, Snake, and Fruit.

I want there to have been a garden where mortality was not a critical issue, where you could love God honestly, without any motive other than love itself, where you could walk with God in the cool of the evening and make love to another human without rancor or hostility or desperation. I want there to have been—and still be—a Garden whose light is so splendid it hides itself.

Although this is like Einstein's searching for a unified field theory, I still think there might be such a place. One writer says Eden was on another planet and that when we were expelled, we went into a spaceship and headed for Earth; we landed on Earth, this author said, when Noah—Adam's last descendant to travel through space—descended from the ark.

I want to find it because my grandmother loved "In the Garden" above all other hymns. She sang it all her life, sang it to me when I was a little girl wondering if I would ever have a winter without an earache. An earache was a big deal in my childhood days, because antibiotics did not yet exist. One of my most persistent memories is of Nana's singing, "I come to the garden, alone" while I lay on the kitchen table, holding my parents' hands as the doctor poured ether onto a washcloth stretched over a tea strainer. As soon as I was asleep, he'd lance my ears, poking holes in my eardrum. And Nana kept singing about the Garden, and I longed to go there so I could have a winter without pain and maybe one where my mother didn't scold so constantly.

Nana's garden was where Jesus walked and talked with you. Even at five or six, I was confused, because as I understood things, Jesus did walk and talk with me all the time, without my having to go anywhere. So I finally figured the "Garden alone" had to be where you could *see* Jesus, where his voice was audible and so sweet the birds hushed their singing. The Garden, the Garden, where everything good was present, and neither earaches nor long division could enter.

That spiritual garden was a splendid place. Nana didn't describe it to me in detail, but she said it had trees, flowers, and birds, all made spectacular by the glowing presence of Christ himself. That radiance I already knew about; after all, the pictures I saw in my slick-paper Sunday school leaflets showed him in garments the whiteness no fuller could equal, and with a shimmering aureole of gold around at least his head and in some pictures, especially those of the transfiguration, encircling his whole body.

Maybe the site of Eden was the place of Jesus's temporary change into the Christ. Probably on Mount Tabor, the hill where Deborah sat under a palm tree judging Israel, known also as the Mount of the Beatitudes and the possible site of the transfiguration. The hill is a continuous garden—flowers, date palms, olive groves, and vineyards still flourish there. The whole hillock is a garden, a Garden in fact, a holy and consecrated place.

My husband and I sat on that hill in the shade of one of Deborah's palms, in the garden outside the Church of the Beatitudes, where a nun gave me a little bookmark with an olive sprig glued in it. We listened to birds we couldn't see, hundreds, maybe thousands of birds, all chirping and caroling. Since we'd been traveling for about four weeks through several countries, we had become cranky and tired, and my husband remarked that they probably had turned on the bird tape to entertain the tourists. But then a flock of tiny yellow and gray birds, finches most certainly, or close relatives, surged out of the trees and darted across and above us, and we shamefacedly gave thanks for all things bright and beautiful.

And the flowers we thrust into the fences at schools where shootings wiped out teenagers, the flowers on the graves of men and women, the flowers in the church, and wedding bouquets and Mother's Day corsages, the lilacs in Iowa, the snowball bushes in Oregon, the desert's yellow-plumed *palo verde*, and the bright poinsettias of Mexico all conspire to make us remember forward. We are remembering what is coming: paradise, a word that comes from the Old Persian *para daeza*, a closed garden, a place where unimaginable flowers on vines hang off walls, and blossoms shoot up beside the golden streets. Remembering forward is why we deck caskets with sprays of roses and surround death with flowers. That is so our loved ones will have blossoms for their journey to the afterlife, flowers to foreshadow the kinds of glorious flowers that grow anywhere you look in heaven.

Meanwhile, God tells me, create a garden on earth—not just the one in my yard that sports fresh-sprung weeds; not the houseplants in my kitchen that sometimes get so vigorous they threaten to hide the pots and pans.

The beds of flowers and edibles I have to create here are, like the kingdom, within me, and they're made from words and deeds. But, God, I said I didn't want to find a metaphorical garden. *So don't find one. Be one instead*, God says, and hangs up before I can argue. God makes it clear that when I snarl at you, I've planted a noxious weed, because you might either snarl back or cringe, neither of which are good ways to live. Likewise, as I take umbrage at every intimation that someone thinks I'm wrong about something, I've robbed the nutrients from the soil.

And if I perform some mitzvah for you or some other member of humankind, if I water my friendships with beneficence and plant seeds of faithfulness, then I am close to Eden. Perhaps at its very gates, perhaps even being allowed past the angel with the sword. I am the steward of the land that is my life, at least until I get to the enclosed garden of paradise, where I know my grandmother is singing still.

Trust and Faith Come Hard

LINDA: I don't think God makes faith easy. Even the Bible isn't clear about everything concerning God, and we only know about a few years of Jesus's life.

KRIS: Maybe God thinks we've got to look at a cross and figure out the rest.

LINDA: Or look at creation and draw conclusions. God's creativity is everywhere, including in us. We are part of creation, so we're God's artwork. But is there a dark side of God? Were the theologians who called God *Deus absconditus* correct?

KRIS: When you say "dark side," do you mean that God is capable of evil?

LINDA: No, but if God is all-powerful, then God permits evil to exist, because it's here.

KRIS: Back to the cross. What about that love?

LINDA: I think deep down, I believe that Jesus died for everyone but me. I can't measure up.

KRIS: Linda! Nobody measures up. As I understand it, believers won't be judged for sin, only for rewards.

LINDA: Well, then, I won't be getting a Happy Meal.

KRIS: [screams softly] Stop it! Why won't you let God approve of you? You don't have to impress God or make God like you, because you're okay just as you are.

LINDA: Then why don't I feel okay with God? I pray and get no results, my sons are wrecking their lives, and my husband is a heart attack waiting to happen.

KRIS: Well, your husband and kids have to work out their own problems. You can't make their lives better once they're grown. I think the purpose of life is to stand still and let God love you.

LINDA: Well, that certainly flies in the face of my Puritan work ethic.

KRIS: I hope so!

LINDA: There's only one way for me to make this work—I've got to quit trying to make it work.

3

THE JIGSAW JESUS

Wrestling with How to Picture God

Unknowing

KRIS: Now we're to the place where our task is separating the image of God from pop culture and the God-petting zoo.

LINDA: I knew this would happen. But I don't want to define God.

KRIS: Maybe we should just talk about what God is *not*. Some religions say God has a human body and human passions. But the God I live with isn't contained in a body. Or anything else.

LINDA: I'd be pretty disappointed if I found out he had a human body.

KRIS: And human passions? That means I could be equal to God. *Some*body's got to be better than I am. I can't be more merciful or loving or just than God is.

LINDA: Not too long ago, I might have tried to describe God. Now I have to take the risk of unknowing.

KRIS: And always wondering if you're doing it.

LINDA: Doing what?

KRIS: Unknowing. It's hard for a pair of intellectuals like us to unknow. It's a deliberate act, and you can't do it for more than a few seconds at first.

LINDA: It would be easier not to define God if we didn't have such constant input from books and TV. You have shelves and shelves of books telling you what God is really like. And all you have to do is listen to CNN and you start deciding what God thinks about our politics or crime or capital punishment.

KRIS: Well, we *can* think about the ways God acts in our lives. The biggest surprise for me was that God has acted as a single parent.

God as Mother

KRIS

Mother and I didn't have a good history. She was beautiful, brilliant, creative, and accomplished. She played Chopin like a master, wrote several books, and illustrated one of them. Mother was full of charm and had many friends; if you met her, you'd think she was delightful and fun. She was also a total narcissist, and we were at war a lot, or at least in skirmishes.

She hated politics and waved away world news. What happened had to, in some way, be about her, and she couldn't control the rest of the planet. So her world got smaller as she aged, smaller and smaller until finally her self-centeredness imploded, fell in on her; and she died somewhere in that state.

When my mother was eighteen years old, she and my father, her future husband, were in a serious automobile accident that sent her through a windshield. Many of her bones were shattered, and her back was scarred by battery acid. Her jaws broke and were wired together, and doctors encased her legs and pelvis in heavy plaster for months. She always had a slight limp and couldn't bend her knees more than forty-five degrees. After about six months, my parents were married in that hospital in Gallup, New Mexico. I was born four years later, when she had a well-developed case of what we would now call post-traumatic stress disorder.

Which would have been expected and treated in most situations. But for Mother, craziness became the Right Way and the rest of us were wrong. The fact that she mentioned "my accident," as she called it, every single day of her life came to be a good thing in her eyes: it kept my father and me from forgetting. He had made the left turn so a speeding drunken driver could come over the hill and hit them broadside, after all, and she was his victim. And she had gone through the valley of the shadow of death to give birth to me, hadn't she? And finally, there was menopause, to which Father attributed a great deal of bad behavior. She said she had started "the change" when she was thirty-six. She had periods until she was sixty, so hers was either the longest menopause on record, or she stumbled through her physical life with a sense of doom.

Mother's world was always smallest when I was in it. She shrank it down so that she and I were almost one person, and she almost squeezed the breath out of me by her desperate neediness for love, love, love. One evening when I was about three, she tried to make me say, "I love you, Mother." I called her Mama, and besides, I felt embarrassed and self-conscious, so I wouldn't say it. She tried to bribe me with cookies. She said, "Shirley Temple would say it." She tried to get me to copy the words, one at a time, when she said them. Finally, she let me go to bed, but she was arch and cold, and wouldn't kiss me good night or tuck me in.

Alice Miller, in *The Drama of the Gifted Child: The Search for the True Self*, said, "The mother gazes at the baby in her arms, and the baby gazes at his mother's face, and finds himself therein . . . providing the mother is really looking at the unique, small, helpless being and not projecting her own expectations . . . this child would remain without a mirror and for the rest of his life would be seeking this mirror in vain."[6]

I didn't have a mirror, but Mother did, and she loved me as her reflection. She never liked me much, however, and as I grew older I somehow learned to display a personality that mirrored her, but while she was preening in her reflection, I became sarcastic and sometimes downright hostile to the wrong people, people who didn't deserve it. Love was what she talked about most, and she was a bottomless pit; once when I was sixteen, when she was complaining about my treatment of her, she said, "And you apparently save all your affection for your sappy boyfriends!"

Well, yes. I enjoyed hugging and kissing a handsome boy who smelled like Old Spice a lot more than hugging her.

I went to Sunday school and church and youth group every Sunday, and we talked about our Father God, which was easy for me. Except for ganging up on me with Mother when she instigated a fight, and letting her get away with emotional abuse—he was in love with her and owed her, because of the accident—my father was a good father, an outstanding father. So I didn't need God as badly as some of the girls who had mean fathers or cold fathers or no fathers. What I needed was a mom who liked me.

I didn't think about God as mother until I was much older, reading the fourteenth-century's Julian of Norwich, who said, "Our Savior is our true Mother in whom we are endlessly born yet we will never come out of him."

Jesus? Jesus is my mother? Then is God my grandmother?

I had to work this out somehow. Scholars averred that God had a neglected feminine side. But furor occurred in England in 1998 when Methodists there published a new worship book that says, "God our Father and our Mother, we give you thanks and praise for all that you have made . . ."

Uh-oh. They called God *Mother*, and millions of very conservative Christians were horrified. Neil Dixon, the secretary of the Methodist Faith and Order Committee, said the prayer "was not an attempt to change the gender of God. . . . But if all human beings are created in God's image then feminine as well as masculine attributes must reflect God's nature."

But in my own case, I had to explore God as my mother. After I read Julian's words a few scores of times, I edged up to God and began to make small, mewing, snuffling sounds. God was the lion this time, and I was a cub, wanting to play, but scared. No big paws had smacked me into a wall or across a yard.

So I reran my childhood, but this time the pain of my earthly mother's tongue-lashings was overcome by Somebody whispering, "It's okay, honey. Don't cry, baby. I love you. I know you didn't mean to be rude to our guests. Hey, kid, all teenage girls yell at their mothers. You're okay." And finally, on my wedding day, "I'm so proud of you, dearest."

I got to replay my whole life and hear that Somebody's voice being gentle and maternal, Somebody gathering me under wings of comfort, picking me up when I fell down, encouraging me when times were hard. Saying things to me that I'd never heard.

Someone said once that the mark of a real mother was her unconditional love and approval. Isn't that a part of God too?

God as Father

LINDA: Well, while you were looking for God's mother side, I was trying to avoid the father side. My own father adopted me when I was three or four, and I know he loved me, but he was very authoritarian.

KRIS: Harsh?

LINDA: Strict. And yes, harsh sometimes. Not physically—he never hit me, but his punishments were legendary among my adolescent friends. Mom would sometimes go in and say, "Now, Jack," to soften the sentence, and other times I would try to sneak around him and his rules.

KRIS: And how did that influence your feeling toward God the Father?

LINDA: I was scared of God and thought I had to be perfect to keep God from being mad at me. I was afraid to confront either my father or God, even when I was angry.

KRIS: When did you learn to separate your dad from God?

LINDA: It's still a work in progress. Old lessons die hard.

KRIS: And do you try to slip past God?

LINDA: Well, it doesn't work, but now I know I don't have to sneak around God.

Breaking Curfew

LINDA

One night in December when I was sixteen years old, my strict no-nonsense dad allowed me to take in a movie with a boy from my school. The two of us had a great time, but it was at least an hour past my curfew before we realized it. The boy said good-bye and drove off as I approached the door to the kitchen. I peeked inside through the window. To my horror, I saw the unmistakable silhouette of my father, sitting on a stool next to the oven. Smoke from a cigarette rose above Dad's head. My teeth chattered as I hung around in the driveway, trying to think of some way past him. No use, though. I knew I was busted.

Dad grounded me for a long while. I learned not only to avoid missing curfew but also not to break Dad's rules. How I added this up to mean that Father God was like my well-meaning but authoritative earthly version has got me into trouble more times than I can count. I've struggled to rid myself of these misperceptions because I want to be homeward bound for God.

For some, a loving Father is the only God they've known. They can't imagine anything else. For the rest of us, going home to God is a little like trying to sneak in late, knowing Pop is hiding in the shadows, eager to catch us in the act of sin. We want to go home—where it's safe and warm—yet we wish we could do it without answering to the Big Guy. Sometimes we stand outside shivering for a long time before we make a run for our room.

The trickster God, the lightning bolt–wielding deity, is a hard idea to shake. Now and then I confess to close friends that I have trouble believing that God loves me, not on a one-time basis—nearly everybody has doubts now and then—but as a constant guiding force in my spiritual life.

I've tried to heal my inner child, done therapy for bad memories, memorized Scripture, and got my head anointed. I've dropped out of church and said some judgmental, mean things about what I thought were repressive people and practices. Sometimes whatever I do to break through the barrier I set up helps for a time. Then I'll go around marveling at God's breathtaking handiwork and seeing miracles everywhere I turn.

But inevitably the doubts return. For me, God once again morphs into a coyote, a creature the Navajo believe is the symbol of trickery. I think I've finally got it and darkness descends again. I may say God loves me (and you and everyone), but my heart disagrees. Usually, a mountain of self-doubt interrupts my journey home to God at about the same time my personal problems decide to grow exponentially.

Of course, I don't have much time for God anyway when I'm trying to put out all these stubborn fires. Delinquent boys, financial constraints, college kids who always need money—it's safe to say my life is a dysfunctional disaster almost all the time. I do my best, but the last thing I want when I'm stressed out and panicked is for someone to sweetly suggest I pray about it.

What? Ask the Big Meanie to bail my sorry self out of trouble? Thank God for no heat on the coldest day of the year and snow in the forecast? Take a chance on the Coyote? What if God's out to get me?

Things go from bad to worse. If God is out to get me, then I must protect myself. I withdraw from God, from church, from community. My head screams, *Fool!* but I separate myself emotionally. I can't forget, much less forgive. God can't hurt me now.

But I hurt myself. Daddy was too stern when I was late, so God must be the same. Unforgiveness gives rise to resentment. Bitterness brews a cruel tea in me. Before I know it, I've cringed like a cornered animal. God and home zooms a universe away. I'm left shivering in the cold.

But God has never left me there. You might think I've simply crossed myself off God's list, end of story. But this is where the real homecoming story begins. Yes, I'm a stubborn person who's been hurt. My childhood image of God isn't ideal. Bad stuff happens to good people. Sometimes life is awful.

I think there must be a switch deep in my brain that suddenly lights up when God, the real one not the phony Trickster, comes running. All I have to do is turn my face toward home, and a loving God dashes out to meet me. Not because I'm good or bad or because I do anything special. Not because God feels sorry for me or needs to punish me for my sins. God greets me with open arms because that's who God really is.

For some of us, homecoming is something that happens more than once. The miraculous part is that with each homecoming it's possible to fall into God's arms as if for the first time. If I ever get to the place where I truly, down deep, through-and-through get this down for good, I'll be amazed. My goal is to erase that childhood God completely. Over and over again I work on it: *God likes me,* I say to myself. *God thinks I'm not only swell but also a personal favorite, has a special place prepared for me,* etc. I may try to revive that irrational concept of a crabby Creator or a dad with a strange way of showing affection.

God as Lover

KRIS: I'm sorry you were so scared of your father. I loved my dad, and I wish he were here now.

LINDA: I miss my dad too. As I got older, we became very close. His strictness was because he wanted to protect me and also because a rule was a rule.

KRIS: But it sounds as if he made up the rules as he went along.

LINDA: That's where the similarity between my father and God end. God's rules don't change.

KRIS: *Really!* How about the difference between the Old Testament God and Jesus?

LINDA: There you go again, pointing out paradoxes and puzzles.

KRIS: Look, if you want to be intimate with someone, you have to see everything about them, including the mysteries. If you fall in love with God, you can't add, "Well, except for . . ."

First Love, Last Love

KRIS

We stood under the porch light, gazing into each others' eyes. We'd spent the evening in a state of exaggerated bliss, ignoring the other people at the party, sometimes squeezing our hands together. We were madly in love, David and I, and we were already talking about marriage.

The only trouble was we were both fourteen.

I couldn't fall asleep at night because David was running through my brain. I could hardly eat, and I believed that the only times I was conscious, really alive, were the moments or hours I was with him.

We of course didn't "date." He came to my house, where we played cards or board games, and we went places with our church youth group. When I wasn't with David, I was thinking about him, remembering our small shy smiles, our hand-holding, and a few quick kisses on the cheek. I can't remember ever being happier than I was during that time. When he and his family moved across country, I felt for a while as if my life were over.

First love is life at its best. Think back to yours. I'm sure there was someone you felt that way about. How long has it been? Try to call up the excitement and happiness you experienced, remembering the waves of warmth and love that washed over you when you looked at him or her. Maybe you even married your first love—but now that marriage may not be what it was when you started out.

Philosophers and theologians have for years spoken about the joys and struggles of first love. Even Jesus.

To find out what he said, take a virtual journey to a city in what is now Turkey. At the time of Christ, Ephesus was a major port, like Rome or Alexandria. The city's Temple of Artemis was one of the Seven Wonders of the Ancient World, and great ships sailed into the harbor every day. Situated on the Aegean Sea at the mouth of a wide river, the city was one of the greatest seaports of the ancient world and the hub of overland trade routes. Ephesus was granted special honors by Rome, which installed many monumental buildings and architectural adornments; and through Roman engineering, the harbor was kept open despite the silting from the river.

A growing congregation of Christians lived in the city, and during that time, St. John wrote his Revelation. In the second chapter he wrote that Jesus, after praising the church in Ephesus for its works, its toil and endurance, and its doctrine, said, "Yet I hold this against you: You have forsaken your first love. . . . Repent and do the things you did at first. If you do not repent, I will come to you and remove your lampstand from its place" (vv. 4–5 NIV).

We can't see heavenly lampstands, but we can see the consequences of having them removed. By late Byzantine times, not so long after St. John wrote down Christ's warning, the bay channel had become useless. Today nothing is left of Ephesus except some broken columns and other ruins, and its famed harbor has filled in with silt from the Cayster River; in fact, the harbor is gone, and its original coastline is six or more miles inland. You can still see the remnants of the coastline in the marshlands, but they are swampy and archaeologists have had to dig through many feet of mud to find what ruins and relics they have uncovered.

A few families and tour guides still inhabit the village, and a number of historic ruins have been exposed. But because the church there abandoned its first love, forgot the freshness of its spirit, a great harbor and an important city disappeared. Jesus didn't warn them that they had quit their Bible studies or their adherence to modesty and morals. He lauded them for their diligence in keeping false apostles outside its walls. But they let their connection to the living God wither and forgot how to do the works of healing and absolution and discipline that were the core of their faith.

Jesus showed us how to keep love active, and he linked that love to eternal life. "Love your enemies," he said, "and pray for those who persecute you, that you may be sons of your Father in heaven" (Matt. 5:44–45 NIV). He reminded us that the greatest act of love is laying down one's life for a friend (John 15:13). And he showed us what to do. The Gospel of John says, "Jesus knew that the time had come for him to leave this world and go to the Father. Having loved his own who were in the world, he now showed them the full extent of his love" (13:1 NIV). He did it by washing their feet and then presenting himself to be crucified even though he was innocent.

Paul preached to the Ephesians, in person and by letter. Writing to the Christians in a city whose architecture was marveled at, whose buildings were among the most beautiful and awe-inspiring in the Roman world, he said, "You are . . . members of the household of God . . . with Christ Jesus himself as the cornerstone. . . . you also are built together spiritually into a dwelling place for God" (Eph. 2:19). But the Ephesians lost their first love, and all their grand construction—religious and architectural—could not make up for the eternal youth they needed in their faith.

And there is our lesson: Keep it alive, keep it fresh, and let it be your first love. That doesn't mean you have to return to childhood

or whenever you first came to Christ. You don't have to start praying "Now I lay me" again to show God you're still a spiritual child.
The symptom of your having that first love, that eternal youth, that
dew-pearled rose is to acknowledge God's making all things new.

If you don't, your faith turns to dust or ashes, like the life of the
pagan prophetess at the shrine in Cumae. She was granted a single
wish by the god Apollo. She was beautiful and she was famous.
Every year hundreds of people journeyed to the temple cave where
she would divine and forecast. She asked Apollo for eternal life, but
she failed to include eternal youth as part of the deal. Wrinkled and
decaying after hundreds of years, she sat in a big open jar that hung
in the temple; and when they asked what she wanted most, she said,
Apothanein thelo, which means "I wish to die." Her soul was emptied,
her wisdom vanished, and she could neither live fully again nor die.
She was destined to exist forever, slowly turning to dust but still
aware, still longing for relief, caught in one moment forever.

Like most ancient Greek myths, the story of the sibyl tells a truth
about our spiritual life: If you don't nurture the free spirit God put
into you, you'll turn to spiritual dust. You have the choice of staying
really alive, or turning into dust. Because to stay alive, you keep your
faith fresh, and you must be willing to put yourself in the hands of
that dangerous God who wants everything.

So repent, as the Revelation says. In New Testament Greek,
metanoia (always translated "repent") means "turn around." Turn
around and go a different way, because the spirit of First Love can
propel you heavenward, giving your life direction and revealing your
spiritual roots. Repent and follow the gang of carnival jugglers and
clowns; turn around and walk to the music you hear in the distance.
Repent and become a fool, a lump of clay in God's hands, a harbor
not hidden by mud, a star winking in the night sky.

Do you remember how you felt when God first came into your
life? Think back. Maybe your adventure with God was a gradual

one, when more and more you found that you believed. Or maybe there was a moment—you were walking in the woods or singing the last hymn at church or listening to someone talk—when you felt Christ move within your spirit. Whichever it was, waves of love swept over you and you thought more about God than about what you were having for supper. Remember the joy, the absolute bliss you experienced every time you thought of Jesus? Remember?

Try to remember your first love for Christ, the rapture you felt, and the joy you knew. If you do, God will probably keep your lampstand in the temple.

Taking the Leap

KRIS: I think that if you can remember your first love for Christ, you'll experience overwhelming grace.

LINDA: Well, grace is risky. You have to let go of any illusion that you're sinless, because grace abounds where sin does. And if you get into a state of grace, you have to trust God to keep you there. To make it more complicated, trust has more than one layer.

KRIS: Let's say you get a sudden dollop of grace. Will that just make you feel loved and worthy, or will grace bring something with itself?

LINDA: Redemption. Joy. Oh, and grace. Grace brings more grace.

KRIS: And Jesus knows how hard life on earth can be. You know that song about what if God was one of us? Well, he is. As Jesus.

LINDA: Okay, Jesus, here I come. I'll take that leap across the abyss and ask for grace.

A Risky Business

LINDA

Like the black holes of science, places in the universe so heavy with gravity that even light cannot escape, my world often feels as if all the light is being sucked out. Divine mercy remains abstract, and I'm embarrassed to admit that my awareness of God flickers with uncertainty and threatens to burn out.

Today I examine my life. I see nothing but holes—unmendable black holes, with rotting edges and shortcomings that go on forever. I've judged people who are probably trying their best. I've helped my grown children long after they needed it, crippling their own growth. My bent toward perfectionism makes me critical and impatient. I've said or thought awful things when those in my world haven't acknowledged how hard life can be for a "one-armed paperhanger" like me. Even God gets an earful; because he could heal my paralyzed arm but doesn't, because he lets me struggle in a household of craziness as my family dances the marathon of substance abuse. The holes in my life succumb to a crushing gravity, and they're growing deeper all the time.

Kristen tells me, "You need a little more of God's grace." I lament that I don't even know what grace truly is. It's a subject every theologian has touched, and I doubt I know anything new.

Of course, I've written about grace before. I've told how in my childhood a Mexican babysitter gave me undeserved breaks and rescued me from near drowning. You'd think I'd remember more about grace in my daily life, but like the Lord's mercies, grace feels new to me every morning. Unlike gravity and other constants, grace never feels like a sure thing. Every day grace challenges me to find it again, to touch my palm to a hot stove and see if I come out alive. Like God, grace is dangerous and irresistible.

And it costs me everything.

I don't mean I think I can earn my way into God's favor—great thinkers from the apostle Paul to modern writers like Philip Yancey caution us not to believe we can make God love us any more or any less than God already does. Undeserved favor means getting a break from God without prerequisite. But God's grace isn't something for nothing. In return God asks me to hand over my life.

For me, surrender means unending questions—to whom am I giving my life, anyway? The God who thinks I'm the best, who rescues me from my own foolishness, who reassures me of love? Or do I cede to that angry God of my childhood, the Gotcha! God who anticipates my every stumble into sin with harsh punishment and no possibility of parole?

Some days I'm none too certain to which version of God I'm giving my all. I'm afraid that risks of grace may cost more than I can give. I'm on a limited budget much of the time, and discount grace sounds appealing.

Dietrich Bonhoeffer wrote that cheap grace is the grace we bestow on ourselves. If I yell at my loved ones, for instance, I can say I'm tired and stressed out or that my hormone level is out of balance. Cheap grace may be no less than a flimsy excuse. If I forget to use my turn signal, yet the traffic cop lets me off with only a warning, one could argue that the policeman was in a forgiving mood. But when costly grace erupts, something outside myself prompts me to help, and not because anyone's watching.

Bonhoeffer asserts that costly (or true) grace condemns sin and justifies the sinner. But don't trot around "sinning merrily" so you can rely on grace to bail you out, he warns.

This pricey version of grace doesn't sound like fun. But it's the only way light will ever penetrate the terrible holes in my life.

To accomplish my surrender to grace, I take the biggest risk of all—I decide to hang my very being on the idea that God's story is for real. I must embrace the cross—complete with all its suffering and redemption. Through the story of Jesus, God risked everything to buy back humanity—and in the process God paid dearly.

Bonhoeffer argues God's grace is "costly because it cost the life of his son—ye were bought at great price. Costly grace is the Incarnation of God. It compels a person to submit to the yoke of Christ and follow him; it is grace because Jesus says, 'My yoke is easy and my burden is light.'"[7]

Martin Luther learned that the price of grace is one's very life and it must continue to cost him the same price every day. Thomas Merton claimed, "I am all burned up with desire and I can only think of one thing—staying in the fire that burns me."[8] Even Kristen, who says I need more grace, says, "If you accept grace, you sacrifice your life. God may destroy the parts he doesn't like, but the exchange is life for eternal life."

If costly grace is worth everything, then count me in. I stride up to the throne and say, "I'll work hard to accept this precious stuff, God. I'll study and pray and squeeze my eyes shut tight to receive grace. I'll hold my breath and deny myself dessert and become really really good, God. God?"

I think God sighs a little here and says simply, "Relax. It's free."

"But you said it's costly," I say, stepping carefully to avoid falling into one of my black holes. "Besides, if you really knew me, God, you wouldn't pass out grace for free. It's supposed to hurt, isn't it?"

Maybe that thunder you hear is heavenly laughter, rumbling across time.

I wonder if God ever gets tired of his children forgetting that grace is like manna, that the costly grace that is so dangerous has to be renewed over and over, that yesterday's grace is rotten and not fit for human consumption. God has to remind me daily of the riddle of grace—it's free; it's expensive. Grace is chancy yet assured, more mysterious than black holes and more unified than any scientific theory. Grace is mine and I can't work to obtain it, any more than I can believe by wanting to. Relax, God says. I'm sufficient for you.

The Lord of sufficient grace says, "Here, have an extra helping of grace. Don't worry that you're a disabled, overachieving, codependent woman, buckling under the weight of middle age and menopause. Do get real about being perfect—and you'll feel better if you judge others a teeny bit less, dear. By the way, I kind of like the things you're doing using only one arm."

Light escapes, bursts out of all the weighty places that have kept it captive. The heavenly hosts break into song. I gasp at the sight of authentic grace and bow to God's elegant invitation. I breathe in the expensive kind of grace, and I didn't have to work for it. But God isn't finished with me.

"Now go and do likewise," God says.

"Me, dispense grace to others?"

"You heard me."

"But, God, I'm so petty. I'm an ugly little judge and crippled to boot." I don't know why I argue, and I don't know why God is so patient when I do. I always picture a bit of eye rolling, until I finally get it. Then God hands out a fresh cupful of light every day and tells me to spread it around.

This light isn't a sunbeam of happiness or a Pollyanna ploy to make people feel better. The grace light goes beyond simple kindness—although kindness is good too—to undeserved favor for undeserving people. God's grace attains escape velocity and exposes the blackest holes. I practice bestowing grace freely, and when I do, I notice I'm being burned alive.

The holes in my life are still horrible, and I frequently forget about the "fresh grace every day" part of the deal. But like Karen Karper, author of *Where God Begins to Be*, writes: "Each event of the day, welcome or not, (can be) an invitation to awareness, a moment of grace."[9]

Relax—grace is free. You can't earn it or save it, bury it or hawk it. Yes, costly grace is risky and you'll pay with your life, just as Jesus did on the cross. Some days you'll miss out on grace because you're in the depths of your own black hole. But practice—practice letting God shower you with unearned mercy and practice showing grace to as many people as you can. The light of grace is unbearable at times, because it's so dazzling and hot. Try not to run away screaming.

I look at my holey life today, and as always, it's a pitiful mess. I need a little more grace than I've got, and not the cheap kind either. I feel like weeping, like telling God I'm unmendable, and besides, I'm mad that God refuses to heal me, physically or emotionally. I don't deserve grace. Do I?

God agrees with me, but says that's not how grace works. God starts at the beginning with me, as usual, and tells me again about why Jesus died and rose from the dead, about how I'm justified, about the cupful of light God gives us every day. Like Karper I'm trying to remember that "the Holy one is calling us to risk all and follow new trails."[10] Rather than burning out along the trail, I want to burn up with the surrender to a risky grace.

God, the Single, Whole Parent

LINDA: Isn't birthing necessary to letting God be the Creator?

KRIS: Okay, let's talk about God the Father.

LINDA: It's helpful to me to think of God as Mother and Father because I have trouble separating our Father from my father, who was authoritarian and not very magnanimous. My earthly father was jealous of me, envious of me. On the one hand, he admired my artistic abilities. When I took my first high school art course as a senior, he asked to hang my first textile project in their bedroom, and he expressed envy, saying he wished he'd done it. He had a degree in art, after all. But he was jealous and possessive with me when I wanted to do something that didn't interest him. When I participated in a drama group, for instance, he shook his finger at me and said, "Now, young lady, if your grades suffer from this . . ." As if my grades ever suffered!

KRIS: And that hurt.

LINDA: He held me up to his standards, and he had to win. He always had a wet blanket ready to throw on what I wanted to do, and that has always colored my picture of God the Father. As if

God's omnipotence meant he had to squelch me to win. But the God I'm getting to know has no wet blankets.

KRIS: Most of my memories of my father are positive. He was a wild man, an engineer and sculptor, creative and exciting. But when I start thinking of God as Father, it's the negative pictures that pop up first.

LINDA: Yeah. Why is that?

KRIS: Well, God does have an Enemy, one who lies to us a lot. This reminds me of the story of the wheat and the weeds, the tares. A farmer sowed good seed, but when the plants came up, weeds were growing with the grain. The servants told their master that he had sown good seed, so where did the tares come from? And he said, "An enemy has done this."

LINDA: An enemy?

KRIS: The Enemy, I guess, because this is a parable about the kingdom of heaven.

LINDA: So did the servants pull the weeds?

KRIS: No. The farmer said they would uproot the wheat along with the tares, so he let both of them grow together until the harvest; and at harvest time the weeds were collected first and burned. Maybe the negative pictures of our fathers that interfere with thinking of Father God have been sown there by an enemy, maybe the real Enemy or maybe just the natural rebellion inside us.

LINDA: We both have a friend who truly believes that Christians shouldn't doubt. I don't doubt on purpose, but it happens.

KRIS: I don't think doubt is voluntary. Faith is.

4

GETTING THE PICTURE

Wrestling with Fear and Doubt

A Sign

KRIS: Deep down, I want a sign to make me hope. I know what Jesus said, but I'm not sure I'm content with the sign of Jonah.

LINDA: I'm always hoping to find something of God in the material world, some outward sign that I can hang on to. Often I end up losing hope by focusing only on things I can see.

KRIS: So why should we keep looking for God if we can never know with certainty what God's really like? Maybe just as we pray for a sign, we'll see Jesus, coming toward us.

LINDA: Crossing over the gap between seen and unseen sounds terrifying. What if my theories about God aren't true? Worse yet, what if they are true? I don't think I can get across the gap without a guide, and I remember a time in my childhood when the sight of Jesus coming toward me might have transported me straight to heaven. I was pretty lonely, and I never in my whole life felt like I was a full-fledged member of anything: school, clubs, choirs, families. I thought I was deformed, so I didn't deserve to be in the club.

KRIS: I wake up every morning feeling like an imposter, even though I can read my name on books and articles. Is feeling like an outsider the human condition? Is it because we know we're not worthy of salvation, not fit to be in the club in heaven?

LINDA: Being an outsider is hard in childhood. Now I feel as if I'm on a deadline and that if I'm outside too long, I might never get in. The door might be shut forever.

Nose Pressed against the Glass

LINDA

In the same hospital I've mentioned, my stays often lasted several months for surgery and physical therapy. When I was nine or ten, the children on my ward still had plenty of time to make friends, play house, and do what girls everywhere do—form clubs.

Paula was the oldest patient on the ward at thirteen—going on fourteen, she reminded us. Paula wore a bra while the rest of us were still in undershirts. She held court from her wheelchair, and other girls buzzed around her like ladies-in-waiting. One day after hospital school she announced, "We should start a club."

"A club," Ellen and Susan cheered. "A club!" Ellen, the only patient besides me who could walk, skipped around Paula. Susan wheeled off in her chair to find a pad and pencil for note taking. I stood by, torn between my envy of Paula and my wish to be included.

"All you have to do," Paula said from her wheelchair, "is pinky-swear the oath."

"What's the oath?" Ellen's face got as red as her hair.

Susan rolled back, clutching a small pad of paper and a pen. "I'm secretary," she said.

103

We formed a circle around Paula. Her chin tipped up like someone who thinks she knows everything. "Promise to follow all the rules and don't tell anyone because it's a secret club."

Ellen asked, "What about Sharon?"

Paula put a finger to her lips. "We can't let just anybody in this club."

I'd been standing beside Ellen. Something about this didn't feel right. I spoke up. "Who's president?"

Paula sniffed. "I am, of course."

"Of course," Ellen echoed. "And I'm treasurer."

"I think we should vote for president," I said, folding my arms across my chest. "And how come Sharon can't join?"

Paula whispered, "Because of her, you know . . ."

I did know. Sharon's movements were jerky and spastic from cerebral palsy.

Ellen and Susan turned to me. "You don't know anything," Susan sneered. "Paula's oldest, so she's president."

Ellen added, "Maybe we shouldn't let *you* in."

I copied their smirks, but my heart registered the keen pain of rejection. I hated Paula for trying to boss me around. I was mad at all of them for picking on Sharon, who couldn't help it that she had cerebral palsy.

In a sudden snap of anger I bit Paula's arm.

"I don't even want to join your club," I huffed. "I wouldn't be in your club for all the tea in China!" I stomped away to the bathroom stall and cried until I couldn't cry anymore.

I loathed Paula and her sidekicks but at the same time I was desperate for friends. Although the situation was unusual—a children's hospital where all the patients had orthopedic surgeries—the battle of independence versus conformity played out in classic fashion. I didn't want to be left out of the club.

My experience is common, whether you're eight or eighty. In belonging we find safety, trust, acceptance, validation. Whether you're a lonely girl in a crippled children's hospital or a newcomer in church, almost everyone wants to step into the circle of acceptance. We all know how much it hurts to be ignored or, worse, cast out.

Nothing matches the empty pain of rejection. Maybe you're afraid to join into fellowship at church for fear someone will find out your husband's an alcoholic or drug user. Maybe you're sensitive and have trouble trusting others as a result of sexual abuse. Maybe a disparity in income, education, or race from the majority keeps you feeling "different." Whatever the reason, something tells you it's too risky to try for club membership. You tell yourself you wouldn't join for all the tea in China. And you may even think you're the only one who's ever felt so snubbed.

Nose pressed against the glass, you long for inclusion while resenting the very ones you're trying to join. The hospital club didn't last long—patients came for surgery and returned home without much notice. That was long ago, but I sometimes still feel like an outsider. When I enter a new situation, old hurts rise up and I can feel unworthy before I ever introduce myself.

I do what most women do when they're first-timers at a church or a new job or any kind of club. I stand around with a big grin on my face and try to pretend everyone's in his or her underwear so I won't die of fright. Then I begin chatting with God, entreating him to make someone talk to me and hurry up so I don't look stupid.

At church I shake hands with greeters after services; maybe wander toward the coffee in the fellowship hall. I'm never sure whether to strike up a conversation with a stranger or sit with my eyes downcast and make note of the different types of shoes that go past. I've never attended a church that didn't welcome me, but at times I've come not only to worship but to become one of the gang.

And if one of the congregation approaches me, what'll I say? Beyond the weather and where I'm from, how many children and my job description, how can I be sure if what I'm saying means anything? I've slunk out many a side door because I was afraid no one would like me. Then I wondered all the way to my car if those who spoke to me were really interested or were only going through the motions of hospitality. Those times a tiny part of me wants to shake the dust from my sandals while most of me wants to be in with the in crowd.

I don't think churchwomen intend to be clannish. Yet lots of us feel the acute pangs of exclusion, either by fashion, status, or—gasp!—even godliness. Jesus dined with sinners and a favorite saying is that it is the sick who need the Physician. Yet addicts, criminals, and other fringe persons are often treated as if they have no place at Christ's table.

If I sit alone in church, not knowing a single person, I can choose to be as stubborn as I once was as a child. I can rail against the cliques of those I consider privileged or whose high status is obvious. I can refuse to play the silly social games and go cry in the bathroom. Or, God forbid, bite somebody.

Or I can dare to think out of the box—or church—to allow strangers to enter my world and take a tentative step toward them. I may find that belonging to this club isn't all that great after all. But in faith communities everywhere, there are many groups with diverse interests. I may unearth pure friendships that bring out the best in Christianity and the best in me. Yet to join the club is to risk that others will find out I'm a big imposter.

While I'm busy reminding myself that no one would ever really love me because my arm is deformed—not just a little too this or not enough that but deformed—God's got the whole choir of heaven shouting down at me, "Not!"

But like an anorexic who sees obesity in the mirror instead of a skeleton, I see a mangled body staring back at me. Never mind about all the normal stuff—I focus on my paralyzed, withered limb and zoom! All I can see is that slightly irregular left arm.

Maybe you feel like an imposter too. Maybe you get up every day and hope nobody discovers your awful secret, whatever it may be. You know you can't hide from God, who sees us as we really are, but you're not going to risk that some person might stumble onto the truth. The Imposter Theory is a dangerous way to live—and it's lonely too.

I write about the imperfections of my life so other imposters will take a chance. People who know me say over and over that they don't see me as being deformed. But that's the way I feel a lot of the time, and it has crippled my self-esteem—that feeling that I too belong. Human beings have a basic need to connect with one another, and I'm no different. We all want to be in the club.

As a nine-year-old crippled kid, I stood with my nose pressed against the glass, longing for acceptance and inclusion—even if it was only a hospital girls' club. When I was rejected, I said I wasn't interested in belonging. How many times since then have I been afraid to show myself, for fear that someone else is smarter, richer, better dressed, thinner, more popular? I've shortchanged myself with deforming self-talk, when no one else saw a problem.

There will always be cliques and in-groups—formed either purposefully or accidentally. I could become a millionaire, get plastic surgery, and go back for my Ph.D., but I could still believe I'm an imposter. Despite any human intervention, my left arm will likely always frustrate me with its limited use and chronic pain.

But I don't have to allow it. Like you, I can hold my breath and dive into God's inner circle. I tell you about being deformed so you won't be afraid to let someone else get close to you. Get painfully real with someone you trust and, yes, you could get burned. But chances are God's going to send that same bunch of heavenly hosts to stay in the way of anyone who would use your secrets against you.

In God's club we all have imperfections. Our bodies are flesh and blood, and our lives on earth a mere moment in forever. No matter if you've an embarrassing past, you're fashion-challenged, or you live with cerebral palsy or a bum arm, remember that membership doesn't depend on outward appearances. God looks inside for initiation into eternity. Belonging is the cry of every heart.

Arguing with God

LINDA: Do you want to get into the club too?

KRIS: Everybody does. As I said before, I think maybe we have a whole society of people who feel like outsiders. But I'm mad at God a lot.

LINDA: Is it okay to question God's ways? I get nervous when it looks like I'm doubting. Is it dangerous?

KRIS: Well, whether you say it or not, God knows what you think. But if I argue, then I obviously believe. I wouldn't argue with the wind.

LINDA: So you *do* love God?

KRIS: Sometimes our relationship gets a little thin.

LINDA: You mean you question God or the Bible.

KRIS: My grandmother, who was four foot nine and weighed sixty-nine pounds, was talking about the "turn your other cheek" command in the Sermon on the Mount. She was such a sweet Christian, but she leaned forward, her blue eyes like forget-me-nots, and said, "You know, I just can't go along with Jesus on that."

Sometimes I Don't Like God

KRIS

I can remember thousands of times when I knew Christ was right there with me, healing, encouraging, and loving. But I can recall others that included frustration with the Divine. Sometimes it's about bad "luck." For instance, my friend's daughter was born with brain cancer and died when she was two, after having horrifying chemotherapy and radiation. If you want to affix blame, you could say that maybe the baby's father or grandmother smoked cigarettes that altered their genetic code, or that the mother lived in a radiation-polluted area, or that she picked a husband whose family had a huge history of cancer. There's always someone you can pile guilt on, but deep down, whether I announce it or not, I blame God.

I am discomfited by the presence of pain and evil in the center of God's creation. I don't really know how God's universe works, no matter how many three- or ten- or hundred-point explanations I hear. I think it's simplistic to blame everything bad on the devil, but I can't tell whether the physical life of our planet is beneficent, neutral, or even downright mean. And although the New Testament shows me a God who is loving and compassionate, the Bible says,

"Who gives speech to mortals? Who makes them mute or deaf, seeing or blind? Is it not I, the LORD?" (Exod. 4:11). Deuteronomy 28:28 threatens: "The LORD shall smite thee with madness, and blindness, and astonishment of heart," while Isaiah 44:24 announces: "Thus says the LORD, your Redeemer, who formed you in the womb: I am the LORD, who made all things, who alone stretched out the heavens, who by myself spread out the earth."

Really? Did you really form the galaxies, Lord? Then why did you make the earth so hard to live on? Why did you leave us to contend with disease and deadly weather and angry people who cause murders and wars?

St. Matthew says God knows about every sparrow's falling, but I want to know if God cares about every bird that a cat devours or about any blue jay that flies into a clear glass window and is killed. I want to know if God intervenes in life or simply observes it, perhaps saying, "Oh, too bad," when cancer consumes a baby, a majestic whale beaches and dies, or a young father drowns while trying to save his seven-year-old son from the river's white water.

And if God intervenes in some cases, what about others? I once heard an evangelist who was using Romans 8:28 say that as soon as you accept Christ, everything that happens to you will be good and nothing will be accidental. Maybe so, in the ultimate equation: At the end of life you can see God's fine hand in your own history. But what about the guy who accepts Christ at the revival and goes outside to find that someone has stolen his car? We still have the problem of evil in a world that we believe God created.

In the movie *Oh, God*, John Denver, the protagonist, asks God, played by George Burns, why he permitted famine, poverty, disease, and crime. God answered, "I don't permit it; you permit it."

And much of the pain and struggle is the fault of humans, of course. The Russian philosopher Nicolas Berdyaev said somewhere that if you are hungry, that's a material problem, but if your neighbor is hungry, the problem is a spiritual one, and I will admit that most tragedies could be controlled or erased by people: famine, epidemics, ignorance, and despair. If a baby in Rwanda or Brazil dies of starvation, people in the First World ought to shoulder much of the blame. War is likewise the fault of people not God, and so are deaths from "natural" disasters if we arrogantly build on the slopes of active volcanoes, on known earthquake faults, or in hurricane belts. But when the innocent die or suffer through no fault of their own, then I find myself shaking my fist at heaven.

I'm reminded of a conversation between two people in the late Joseph Heller's novel *Catch-22*. Yossarian, the protagonist, tells a woman he doesn't believe in God, and she says she doesn't either; but after a tirade against the Almighty, she starts to weep and hits Yossarian in the head with her fists. He asks why she is so upset, since she doesn't believe in God to begin with.

She replies, "But the God I don't believe in is a good God, a just God, a merciful God." We are loath to think that any God, even a nonexistent one, could be a malefactor, a blind being, a neutrality who lets the chips fall where they may, including on two-year-old babies.

So some days I don't even like God, and loving One who lets creation suffer feels paradoxical at the least and deranged at the most. But I guess I'm hanging on because I keep praying. And because I need God.

St. Thomas Aquinas's five arguments for the existence of God included proof by contingency; that is, because God is necessary, God must be. And even the sardonic Voltaire said, "If there were no God, it would be necessary to invent him."

Efim Sversky, a Jewish theologian, said in his audio book *Connection*: "If God did not want us to contact Him, He would have arranged the world in such a way that we would not suspect His presence nor have the ability to find out about it."[11] Somehow that simple statement comforts my heart and becomes a sign, a proof, an excitement.

But that kind of "proof" also makes my heart ache because it suggests that since human beings have such a need to believe, God condescends to be, to let us believe in divine good; or that although such a kindly God doesn't exist, we have to pretend or we'll go mad. That's not enough for me, and I know too many atheists who haven't lost their minds. But the thought of all humankind going crazy doesn't scare me half as much as the thought of leading my own life without God.

Without God, I would have nobody to pray to, and without prayer, I would be overwhelmed by the challenges and demands in my life. I would feel like the man who, clinging to a bush after falling off a precipice, prayed for help. When God's first instruction was, "Let go of the bush," the man thought awhile and asked, "Is there anyone else up there?"

Well, I wonder if there is. My choices are apparently either to admit God doesn't care and lets us struggle in a poisoned world, or to pretend God is all good and that we'll understand it all some day when we get to heaven. Hmmmph. Heaven is a long way off. Today I'm trying to write and cope with a bad backache, I recently had to have my doggy put to sleep, and I've been struggling with cellulitis, or blood poisoning in my leg, for more than three months. Today I'm horrified by the news on CNN, and my cleaning woman has, as usual, hidden my kitchen implements so I'll have to go on a hunt for my silicone spatula, which will probably be in a coffeepot or under the knives.

So today I'm not sure how to think of God. I have to look deep inside myself, reach for the ideas that are hidden in the darkness behind my heart, and find out what I think, not with my brain but with whatever organ or sense that supports faith. And sure enough, as mad as I am today at God and the government and my cleaning woman, in that dark place I find myself almost bursting not only with belief but with love. I doubt that anyone can look at the cross of Christ and say God doesn't care. Not for long, anyway. The sacrifice Christ made that spring day outside the walls of Jerusalem made it clear how much God cares. Now I wish I could sort out what we human beings are supposed to do for one another and what we can depend on God for.

And ultimately, I guess, that is the purpose of human life: to attend to every matter we can and to trust God for the rest, which sounds an awful lot like Reinhold Niebuhr's "serenity prayer," now used by most 12-step programs. And I have to admit the prayer is meretricious. Accepting the things I cannot change means inculcating in myself the trust that God will, in the end, do it right. I guess I just wish God would tell me what's really going on. It isn't easy to trust the Unseen, especially since most of the time he is also the Unheard.

If the things you can't change hurt too much, you might abandon God. My friend whose two-year-old died got a divorce, quit the church, and says she doesn't believe in God. Do I? I wonder if I'm kidding myself about the whole thing.

I lean back in my desk chair and watch the goldfinch war going on outside my office window. I've never seen anyone get hurt, but they do a lot of fluttering; they peck the air as warning and jockey for position on the black thistle feeder. Goldfinches know what to do. They don't try to be cats or swallows or trees. And they apparently don't wonder about God. They simply know; the matter was settled before they hatched.

And maybe before I came into the world too. I can say the whole thing is a myth or wishful thinking; but the goldfinches and the Hubble photographs and the wind's singing through the Douglas fir woods behind my house all signal that God is present and God is good. Stardust in my bones, leftover after creation, proclaims that

God is good. The stir I feel behind my breastbone echoes the signal, and somehow, even my intellect joins in the chorus. God is good, a good shepherd, a good Father, and for those who didn't have the kind of mother they needed, God is a good mother.

And the bad stuff? Maybe our information is wrong. If we love the streams but hate the dead bodies of water rats, maybe what came from the devil isn't the rotting but the revulsion. Composting is a phase of life, so hating it must be the sign of my fallenness.

But what about the child who was born with cancer and never saw her third birthday? Because of her I have to believe there's more. I have to believe she's in God's bosom, singing with the angels and elders, and maybe, just maybe, she's even praying for me to have a clearer faith.

What Do You Say to an Atheist?

LINDA: Okay. You get mad at God and I get scared, but we both believe. But what about people who don't just reject God but claim there is no God?

KRIS: Do you wonder why they're atheists, or whether they're going to hell?

LINDA: But what do you say to an atheist?

KRIS: Well, "How do you do?" is sometimes appropriate. Or how about, "Fool, can't you tell that God is working all around you?" or "Tell me about it." That usually works for everything.

LINDA: The first time I met someone who said she was an atheist, it caused me to take a closer look at my own faith, to weigh what and why I believe. I was surprised at how I reacted . . .

My First Atheist

LINDA

aith had never come up before in my weekly writer's group. I write faith-based as well as secular works, but I usually don't bring the "religious stuff" to these meetings. I usually run spiritual writing past a Christian group I belong to. I think of myself as a writer who is Christian not as a Christian writer.

Before anyone skewers me for being a poor witness, I know I walk a fine line. I never lie about what I write. But sometimes the urge is strong. The day I met my first atheist, my spirituality collided with the world.

Sure, I've known my share of agnostics and truth seekers—some who've had bad experiences in church, others simply eager to explore other religions. I'm a Boomer from the sixties, after all. My "secular" group prides itself on welcoming diversity—members include lesbians; a divorced, nonpracticing Catholic; a couple of New Agers. I'm the only Christian.

As one of the members of my secular writer's group, I respected "Rita's" insights on how to improve my work. She seemed skilled and honest. Then one day she said something shocking. She sighed and tucked a wisp of hair behind her ear. "I can't critique this essay," she said. "I'm an atheist."

I was flabbergasted. I'd never met an atheist before.

I was dying to ask why Rita couldn't comment on my essay, which was about making peace with God. I'm not sure she understood that I wasn't interested in her opinion about spiritual matters. I wanted hard-nosed pointers on grammar, syntax, and theme. Somehow, though, my mention of God stopped her and she couldn't see past the "G" word. I felt like saying, "Wow, you don't look like an atheist."

Madalyn Murray O'Hair, an atheist who challenged prayer in schools all the way to the Supreme Court, may have influenced my notion of the quintessential doubter. I've always pictured atheists as irascible people with few morals and a skeptical need to measure every detail about life. I've thought a disbelief in the supernatural and distaste for superstition underlined their position. I confess that in my mind's eye they usually sport perpetual frowns and bad hair.

Rita is nothing like my stereotype. She's creative and witty, and her hair looks great. She isn't the least bit unpleasant. But her position as not only an unbeliever but also a nonbeliever sent me on a quest to defend my own faith.

I'll admit her declaration upset and intrigued me. I was a bit ruffled because I asked for a little editing, not a philosophical debate. Beyond the surprise of her reply, I wondered how she arrived at her conclusion that God doesn't exist. Had her life been so full of misery that she couldn't imagine a loving God in control? Maybe God remained silent when she pled for answers. Or maybe she grew skeptical because God can't be scientifically proven. It wasn't an appropriate time to grill Rita, but I left the meeting knowing God wasn't going to let the incident pass—for me, anyway.

In the sixties and seventies I too explored other spiritual paths— paths that sometimes danced me perilously close to the occult. I called on inner gods, visualized health and wealth, and meditated on love. For several years I outright rejected Christianity and embraced an odd cult that combined Jesus with Science of Mind and other metaphysics, as well as a smattering of the supernatural. During those times I was more apt to accept a Buddhist teaching than a Pentecostal principle, but I never stopped believing in God. But then, knowing a real atheist, I had to ask myself what I did believe and why.

My faith pitted against atheism forced me to think about what I truly believe. I was propelled back to the early 1980s, when I clerked in a Bible bookstore in La Mesa, California. This was after my cult membership, when I was finally born-again, thanks to the diligence of my little sister and who knows how many prayers for my salvation.

Behind the register, a rack of books stared at me from their places. *Know What You Believe*, one title admonished. Know what you believe? I didn't even know *why* I believed yet, although I'd renounced all the cult stuff and sold all my metaphysical and occult books. I still felt guilty for being tolerant of other faiths, ashamed for not knowing the words of a good witness. Like the books and a spinning rack of tracts—small pamphlets meant as witnessing tools—I felt inadequate to explain what I believed and why I believed it.

I'd been instructed that Christians should be prepared to explain their beliefs, in case the perfect nudge of the Spirit offered the opportunity to share the Good News. Except that the whats and whys of my belief were still in their infancy then, and the only good news I had was that I'd "accepted Jesus into my heart as my personal Savior." How original!

Over the next twenty-five years I read many Christian apologists, from C. S. Lewis to Karl Barth, Frederick Buechner to Josh MacDowell. I've been searching for an eloquent answer to bolster my meager faith. Theologian Kenneth Prior writes: "If we are to argue our case effectively not only do we need to be masters of what we believe and why, but we must also appreciate the outlook and problems of those we are trying to reach. Otherwise we are in very real danger of talking at cross purposes."[12]

Mastery of belief hasn't come easy for me—but my core conviction, in God as Creator, in Jesus as God Incarnate, has never wavered. I've had to run from the everlasting arms to be enfolded by them and study other faiths to recognize Christianity for what it is. Even when I was involved in the peril of that wacky cult, I sensed that the living God could be equally dangerous—if I dared to allow him full access to my life.

At times I balk at giving God free rein. When terror, death, suffering, and loss create global havoc, any sane person has to wonder what God's thinking.

The Bible forms another segment of my belief. Scripture tells of the one true God who sacrificed his only Son Jesus to redeem mankind. Whether I think the Bible is the Word of God or the words of God, the Old and New Testaments are part of the way I understand the world.

The third basis for my belief comes from the community that surrounds me. I seek diversity in my friendships, but I also find myself drawn to those who are active in the church. As much as I've tried to avoid church attendance, claiming it was boring or too this or too that, these days I'm knee-deep in a congregation that welcomes me.

This faith community doesn't sugarcoat God or condemn him for inventing phlegm. Services celebrate the existence of God and the death and resurrection of Jesus with joy and tears and awe. The what and whys of my beliefs come into focus each time the bells chime at communion, each time I humbly partake of the bread and wine.

So far everyone I've met there admits God does mysterious things; God is a puzzle; God can be silent when we need him; God doesn't act when we think he should. But in the midst of so much uncertainty, we all agree on one thing: God is.

I suppose that for Rita, God isn't. I can't help feeling sad for her and I can't imagine what atheists must go through. For me, life without God sounds as cold and distant as deep space, lonely as solitary confinement, empty as existence without meaning. I'm not going to shove evangelical tracts at her, and I doubt she wants to hear the story of my born-again experience. I pray for her, ask God to show himself to Rita, but I'm not sure what else to do besides love her—and give her unbiased feedback on her writing.

Yet questions about my first atheist lead straight back to my own heart. Twentieth-century philosopher-theologian A. H. Hartzog said it better than I can: "The naked shock rolls over us, the flames burst around us, misery calls out from its agony, sin erupts, and hell breaks loose, but the ship of the Eternal Counsel is brought safely to harbor through the ravage of the storms. The sun rises and sets, rivers flow through the valleys, flowers burst forth from the earth, and the power of love radiates into the open heart."[13]

A Walk on the Wild Side

KRIS: Even if you grow up in a quiet, orderly, controlled household, your spirit can still be wild and free. The parent of that spirit had to be God.

LINDA: I never ran wild and free. From my childhood on, I was an adult in my house, the one who obeyed and got good grades and saw to it that nothing upset my mother.

KRIS: But didn't you yearn to be a bird or a wolf or a cougar so you could escape?

LINDA: I think I wanted to be something that could pull its top down so nobody could find it. Like a trap-door spider.

KRIS: Eeew.

LINDA: I don't like spiders, either, but the burden of my goodness was like your childhood burden of prayer. I wanted a hiding place.

KRIS: What about the hospital? Did you hide there?

LINDA: Are you kidding? I was afraid of God and the nurses and the hospital schoolteacher. I had to please them.

KRIS: I was pretty good through childhood, but every now and then I had to trot into the spiritual woods.

Raised by Wolves

KRIS

We've heard it in television commercials. People do something foolish or gauche or risky, and their friends say, "Were you raised by wolves?"

Well, yes, if you're talking to me.

I was raised and watched over by a great silver Wolf whose eyes flashed fire and who led me into deserts and forests and holy places. The same Wolf who stood beside Barrington Bunny's dead body all Christmas day, and who must have called the little rabbit's soul into heaven,[14] sometimes ran between me and my mother and stood against my body so her words couldn't slay me. Sometimes he sent a Wolf Woman to lick my hands and face and to keep me warm, and once in a while he even let me run with the pack for an afternoon.

The Wolf who raised me was passionate in his concern. Sometimes he scared me: I'd open my closet door and there he was, his eyes and nose all I could see in the dark; he was watching and waiting. At other moments he wounded me, taking my wrist between his teeth and leading me out of destructive situations even when I resisted. But at other times he lay against me and nuzzled my foot, occasionally inviting his whole posse to sleep on my bed. And he kept me in the Way.

The Wolf Way is a spiritual path where you can run and run, always toward the throne of God. If you're willing to become a wolf yourself, you may see divine wonders, drink from consecrated waters, and walk through fires untouched. A spiritual wolf is not a werewolf, which is a victim of dark magic and the moon; spiritual beasts are human beings who willingly have gone to ground in their search for God.

Spiritual wolves protect the innocent, snarl at evil, and howl when Christian truths are wounded or killed. Wolves don't care about charm or self-love or social acceptability outside the rules of their pack. They feel entitled to hunt when they're hungry and fight when threatened. To paraphrase C. S. Lewis's words about Aslan the Lion, my silver Wolf isn't a tame wolf. He doesn't perform or do magic tricks or wear a tutu while pushing a baby carriage, nor is he inclined to do my bidding. In fact, he expects me to obey him.

I'm sure my parents' friends said that I was a child who followed a wolf. Of course, their actual words were that I was unusually creative and inventive, but I heard one of them whisper, "I'll bet she has a wild streak."

We misuse the phrase "wild streak" when we refer to people. What is wild isn't destructive or drunken or criminal. Wild means natural, which is the way God made things. A little girl whose companions are wolves or lions or eagles will not learn evil from them; in fact, she may imitate their nobility and their temperance. They are creatures that don't make war on their own kind or kill more than they need to eat; even a lioness who brings down a wildebeest lets hyenas and scavenger birds take what she and her family don't eat. So if my mother's friends thought I had a wild streak, a wolfian streak, what I wanted was to run free, to be who God made me to be, to pursue an authentic natural life.

And if you're raised by wolves, you hunt all the time. Your nose is to the earth or sniffing the air while you seek new ways to paint or dance or write or worship. You creep close to bonfires in the night, needing the warmth but trying to avoid the fire makers. You howl when you're lonely or when you're trying to locate other wolves or when you just feel like yipping and yowling for reasons known only to yourself.

I don't own the great silver Wolf. In fact, when I was a frantic young mother who yelled at and hit her children, the Wolf stood between my daughter and me, this time protecting her not me. I hadn't abandoned the Wolf Way, but I was moving so slowly it was imperceptible, and falling down more often than walking or running.

Barry Lopez, who has spent most of his writing life studying the relationships between human culture and nature, said, "The wolf exerts a powerful influence on the human imagination. It takes your stare and turns it back on you. (The Bella Coola Indians believed that someone once tried to change all the animals into men, but succeeded in making human only the eyes of wolves.)"[15]

And indeed, we are both enchanted and terrified by wolves. Sheep keepers despise them and want licenses to shoot them in Idaho and Montana, where wolves thrive in repopulation programs. Naturalists and earth mothers, on the other hand, want wolves to roam free in all our forests and national parks. The wolves, however, haven't said anything, but they stare at us.

To shake free of the wolf metaphor, I have to say Christ was most active in my life at the times, at the very moment, when I thought all heaven had deserted me. When I was a little girl, God sent angels in the form of friends and teachers and books. And when I felt dissolute, scattered, and unproductive, God threw the Bible at my head in a new way, so that I had to read it, had to understand it in new ways.

Only in looking back do you realize how much of the time God has wept with you or protected you or nudged you to go on.

The very wildness of Christ is what kept me alive and active through difficult times; he has human eyes, indeed, but the rest of him is something Other, something that can penetrate walls and ascend into heaven. I want to follow him wherever he goes; sometimes I fall down, sometimes I get hurt; but I can always catch his scent, find his tracks. Jesus the silver Wolf makes tracking him easy if I have the will. And I do. I want to disappear into his same cloud and sit at the table at his wedding supper.

But, someone is asking, what about the Big Bad Wolf? How do you know when the creature is God?

Let's suppose the Big Bad Wolf was the personification of evil and that the Three Pigs (and Red Riding Hood and other foolish characters) were ill equipped to deal with him alone. We do have bad wolves and maybe even the Big Bad Wolf striving constantly to eat us up, and because we can't overcome evil by ourselves, we have to put our faith in the real Wolf who will defend and protect us.

There are big bad men and women, big bad dogs, big bad birds. We could probably find big bad plants or rocks if we were really interested in looking for evil. But since God is our sure defense, the one who will not let the waters cover us nor the flames devour us, we will not lose the war with evil, and what is Big Bad will fade away before the glance of Christ.

Now the great silver Wolf walks beside me, occasionally nipping at my heels to keep me on the path or growling softly to call my attention to something. The Wolf Way is the path of justice and compassion, a hunting party with salvation as its object, and a walk through the merciful, unbalanced, joyful Spirit of God.

Seeing God on the Road

LINDA: Buddhists say that if you see the Buddha on the road, kill him. What they mean is that you can't worship someone or something you can see, that your knowledge of God has to come from inside.

KRIS: Okay, but millions of people are putting their faith in shrouds and relics and expeditions to find Noah's ark. God hides the truth inside us and doesn't want us to worship anything external. There's a reason why God hid the burial place of Moses.

LINDA: God didn't want it turned into a tourist trap. But what about physical evidence? Don't we need to know that what's in the Bible is historical fact?

KRIS: Maybe. So then the Garden Tomb and the Church of the Holy Sepulcher are both the empty tomb of Jesus.

LINDA: I haven't been there, but I'd probably agree with you—if only because the God I believe in is bigger than any place. God transcends place. And time.

KRIS: Well, then, maybe neither of the tombs is the one. Maybe biblical archaeology is just a search for proof because our faith in an invisible God is weak. Why do we want graves and bones and arks to prove God is real?

LINDA: Because we are flesh and blood. Matter seeks matter. We want to see something that's like us. Michelangelo painted God to look like a white-bearded man who represents humanity as well as divinity.

KRIS: But we looked like God in the Garden of Eden. According to Jewish legends, Adam was originally both male and female. Maleness and femaleness together is the true image of God, which is why sex is holy.

LINDA: But I still want to know if the image of God needs to be seen by human eyes and felt by human hands. I feel an inclination to want to touch Jesus's garment, just like anyone else. At the same time, I know that my attitude leads to superstition. Magic.

KRIS: You do see and touch the image all the time. God is present right now, as we talk to each other, in our dialogue and our physicality. Maybe to see God, you need to look at a marriage, which is a picture of God re-completed in us.

LINDA: So I don't have to stand on the Interstate and thumb a ride to visit God? I don't have to see or touch the Shroud of Turin to know that Jesus Christ died and was resurrected?

KRIS: Well, if you see God on the road, shut your eyes. God is inside you and outside you and all around. Sartre said, "Hell is other people," but I know God is contained in the love of people for one another.

5

ENTERING THE MAZE

Wrestling with Hope from Within and Without

The God Spot

LINDA: Are humans created with a space only God can fill? The minute disaster slams into your life, you put in an emergency call to God and pray you don't get voice mail.

KRIS: You need to get tough with God, Linda.

LINDA: When I do need help, God does know how to delegate. God nudges people to deliver whatever I need.

KRIS: But deep down, don't you wish God would do it himself?

LINDA: God *is* doing it. There's a reflection of God in everyone, isn't there?

KRIS: I sure hope so.

LINDA: Real hope isn't in a fairy-tale ending but in the promise of eternal life.

KRIS: Linda, if I stopped hoping for a fairy-tale ending, I'd die of grief. And as you said, I think humans are created with a space only God can fill. That's the perfect, happy ending. The God Spot tells us stories that can come true.

Hardwired for God?

KRIS

When I enter my church on Sunday mornings, something happens to me. I kneel to say my first prayers of worship and literally feel the whole week's weight sliding off my shoulders and back. I don't just feel something, I know something. I know it for at least an hour on Sunday mornings and any other time I quit thinking long enough to notice that God is nearby and engulfing me. How do I know? Because my God Spot tells me so.

Blaise Pascal, a seventeenth-century physicist, mathematician, and Christian philosopher, said all humans have a God-shaped vacuum within. Now we have found that vacuum. Scientists at the University of California at San Diego have identified a region of the human brain that appears to be linked to prayer and spirituality. Their findings suggest that we as a species are hardwired, genetically disposed, to believe in God. God is more dangerous than we thought, bent on consuming us, popping up in our brains and nerve endings and involuntary thoughts.

Or is it really God?

Studies of people with temporal lobe epilepsy have found that they sometimes report divine encounters and fearful visitations from other realms. Recent tests of electrical activity in the brain showed that the same area that lights up during a seizure also flared when the subjects thought about God.

Well, then, is faith just a mild form of epilepsy, and God the product of electrical misfires in the brain? We need to know whether the human mind has been touched by God, or if God is an invention of the mind. Which came first, the Spirit or the brain?

This is worrisome, and we wonder if finding out about the religion center of the brain means that we invented God, that faith rose out of primitive humanity's need to explain natural events or to appease forces like storms and earthquakes or to grant continuity to people who have died. The thought that Jesus Christ rose out of folklore, that the resurrection was at best an error and at worst a lie, is so painful that we are cut by it to the heart.

All this could drive me crazy, because I am not only a woman of faith, but I'm also a woman who respects science and mathematics and inquiry. I hate it when science rips away faith and I hate it equally when religion ignores scientific evidence. When Galileo announced the Copernican theory, the church reacted predictably, if not sensibly. Nobody wants God or the universe reduced to a mechanistic principle, any more than we want science to be cast into an adversary position. It turns out that Galileo was right, which makes the thought that science could expose us Christians as people with overactive parietal lobes even more threatening. I tremble to think that science might call the joy I experience in prayer nothing more than a genetic program, a punch in my physical tape.

But with work and prayer, I can embrace both camps. William James, who was born in 1842 and died in 1910, argued that religious states are not less profound simply because they are physical. He said that to insist that the body causes a religious state of mind was "illogical and arbitrary." Because if that were the case, "none of our thoughts and feelings, not even our scientific doctrines, not even our disbeliefs,

could retain any value as revelations of the truth, for every one of them
... flows from the state of the possessor's body at the time."[16]

Although James made his comments more than a hundred years
ago, his commonsense view is still valid. So is that of C. S. Lewis,
who said somewhere that if his thoughts were nothing more than
the movement of atoms in his brain, then he had no reason to believe that he had a brain or atoms moving in one. To glibly dismiss
spiritual activity as a conditioned trick of the brain is the same as
to tell yourself the stars are flat lights on a hard surface.

Tibetan Buddhists were the first group without epilepsy to be
tested and scanned. Their parietal lobe "God Spots" are lighted up
most of the time, perhaps because they spend much time in prayer
and contemplation. During meditation, that lighted area spread
and deepened in these subjects. Practicing Quakers sometimes have
identical brain scans as those of the Buddhists. Catholics' "God
Spots" shine when they say the rosary. And you undoubtedly have
that same kind of brain activity when you pray for your family and
friends or read Scripture or think about God.

That spiritual hot wire, that God Spot, is a small lump of gray
matter nestled in the top of the rear section of the brain, called the
posterior superior parietal lobe. It's also the part of the brain that
keeps track of where you are in physical space, that knows which
way is up and down, right and left, the place that helps you know
whether you're upright, lying down, or standing on your head, and
makes you aware of where you are in your environment. I am at this
moment upright, sitting in my black leather desk chair in front of
my computer, and when I stop to read, I lean forward on my left
elbow. How do I know? My brain tells me so. And now I am also
aware when that brain goes into God Mode.

When George Frederick Handel was writing the "Hallelujah Chorus" in his oratorio *Messiah*, he said he thought he saw the gates of
heaven opened before him. He was flooded with light and awe and

wrapped with grandeur. Handel had just clocked in on his God Spot. John Wesley reported that his heart was "strangely warmed" during a church service at Aldersgate; he launched a movement that became the Methodist Church. The experience of the warm heart was God's implant in him, and Wesley paid attention. And when sinners, unbelievers, turn to Christ, when they are converted, they have allowed the hot spot to operate in their lives. They've given in to God.

Spirituality and Health magazine ran an article in February 2004 with a title that was the redo of a popular antidrug slogan. "This is your brain," says the big print beside the PET scan of a brain. Then, "This is your brain praying" accompanies the photo of a second brain scan, in which the parietal lobe is the orangey-yellow color of autumn sunshine. The brain doesn't originate prayer; something—a need, an invitation, desperation—drives you to prayer, and your brain activates that prayer, turns it into something your nervous system recognizes and responds to. And apparently that something is what God recognizes, because we keep receiving blessings.

All this is the very heart of the dangerous God quandary, because God makes us intelligent and religious at the same time, teases us with PET scans on the one hand and the story of Jesus on the other. Yet you apparently have no choice about that relationship because you have a God-shaped vacuum located in your brain. Since God has apparently hardwired you, you won't have any peace until you open up, surrender, give in, and let your brain light up with warm amber light.

And I looked, and, behold, a whirlwind came out of the north, a great cloud, and a fire infolding itself, and a brightness was about it, and out of the midst thereof as the colour of amber, out of the midst of the fire.

Ezekiel 1:4 KJV

Getting God's Attention

LINDA: Scientific theories like being hardwired for God may help some people to accept God. But what about when you're desperate for answers? Surely we don't plead with God solely because our brain chemicals tell us to do so. There must be more to it than that.

KRIS: Marcus Borg writes about human intuition as being more than a hunch. For me, God is deeper than something humans can measure. So I've got the God Spot and the Bible and my intuition and the church.

LINDA: [sighs] Seems like I've spent my whole life trying to get God's attention.

KRIS: Sounds like you need a direct line to God.

LINDA: That's the problem. If I call, will God answer?

Pick Up, God

LINDA

Today I'm so sick with worry I could die. One of my grown sons, a "lost boy," is in deep trouble. At twenty-five, he's not really a boy anymore and neither is he lost. Over the past few months he's gotten a good job and a pay raise and been named Employee of the Month. We all thought his life was finally on track. His phone call from the county jail to say he's been accused of a serious crime punched me in the gut. He claims he's innocent.

I believe him. He says his employer's surveillance tapes will prove he was working at the time of the crime. While I have no evidence that any of my friends would gossip, I'm still afraid to tell a single person about this awful situation. My extended family has already passed judgment on my son's alternative lifestyle. Why won't he quit skateboarding? How can he sport those awful piercings? Some of my loved ones have already taken a stand. I can't risk the shunning that sometimes occurs when human foibles become public knowledge.

So I dial God's number, over and over—pick up, God.

The Jesus image in my mind stares at me with sympathy, but says nothing. Scriptures float across my thoughts: *Do not be afraid. Lo,*

I am with you always. With God nothing shall be impossible. Cast your cares upon him for he cares for you. Lots of words that try to cover a mother's gaping wound.

I tell myself that I can trust my Christian friends to do the right thing if I ask them for prayer. Can't I? I admit that I've recoiled from persons with unsavory backgrounds. I'd probably cast a stone along with the worst hypocrite if I thought I had to avoid association with riffraff. I've attended Bible studies and women's groups where prayer requests were little more than the religious version of the grapevine. So I conclude that it's too perilous to name this dire circumstance to anyone, even my most trusted sisters in Christ.

Pick up, God. Please answer. I know you're there—why won't you talk to me? Here's a mystery: The God who created everything, who is Lord of all and who is love itself, is so often quiet when we humans face desperate moments. I don't know the answer to why God remains hidden in troubled times, but I sometimes wonder if God desires us to console one another instead of relying solely on the invisible Divine. Whatever God's true motive for not clearly revealing his presence, it's too dangerous to confide in anyone except God right now, although every cell in me screams for the release and comfort of a sympathetic ear.

Maybe I'm wired for companionship. I need comfort, a need that my husband doesn't share. He wants no one to know about our son's problems—and I will respect his wishes as a sign of unity. I guess he feels compelled to keep crises to himself.

My younger sister, Leslie, who first led me to Christ, also retreats when things go wrong and is generally very private. She runs into her prayer closet in times of trouble and dialogues with Jesus. Lots of times I don't know about dire circumstances in her family until long after they occur.

But for some reason, I need a shoulder to cry on—one with skin. My first instinct is always to pick up the phone and wail to my best friend. But this time, I can't. Not right now. In the absence of any person to pour out my troubles to, the silence is deafening.

God? I stare into a mirror and see only my tear-stained face.

I try to compensate by comparing. My troubles aren't earthshaking. Thousands across the globe succumb to hunger and disease every day. Tribes and factions annihilate each other over territory, while the world chokes slowly beneath the haze of global warming and human intervention. What's a little scrape with the law compared to a loved one writhing in the agony of cancer's final stages? When I put my situation into perspective, all of humankind shrinks to an infinitesimal size. But my pain is real. Another familiar verse wafts in on a gentle summer breeze: "Are not two sparrows sold for a penny? Yet not one of them will fall to the ground apart from your Father" (Matt. 10:29). So I know God's aware of the problem. Comparison leads to a dead end.

Then I try "naming it and claiming it." If I claim victory in Jesus's name, I can name the best possible outcome for my son. Well, what was victorious about my father's death a few years ago, when I told myself to "name and claim" a miracle cure for his terminal kidney disease? That day, affirmations melted into tears. I don't tend to be a pessimist but in my father's case it was overly hopeful to expect a miraculous healing. Dad died, despite medical technology and loads of "claiming the victory" prayer. I know healings do occur, but in my father's case no miracles ensued.

What about God's will? I search for places in my life that need cleansing and I repent, lest prayers for my son bounce against the ceiling. I know God needs to touch him and I know he needs God. Yet if he's truly innocent, I find it difficult to believe God's will is to ruin his life with prison and who knows what else.

If I apply that logic to my own physical disability, then it must be God's will for me to live with chronic pain. My mind won't fit around the concept of a God who inflicts injustice on the innocent any more than I can accept a God who dispenses the plague.

Reading the Bible comforts me, but what I really want is for God to break open the prison doors the way he did for Paul when he was imprisoned. I'm trying my best to feel God speaking to me through the Scriptures, but what happens if my eyes fall on some awful verse in Leviticus, where a son could be stoned for disobeying his parents?

Using well-known slogans isn't much help either. While I admit I've said, "God closed a door but opened a window," I have no way to prove God did anything at all. What if coincidence plays a bigger role in my life than I care to recognize? I want to believe that good triumphs over evil, that if my son is indeed not guilty, he'll be exonerated, but if that's true, then why is there a need for the Innocence Project, a legal aid center cofounded by attorneys Barry C. Scheck and Peter J. Neufield? The Project has freed hundreds of falsely convicted prisoners in this country, mostly through the technology of DNA evidence. The kinds of circumstances that convict the wrong man are so egregious that God couldn't be behind such terrible situations.

Finally, what about calling on the Holy Spirit? I do believe in the Comforter, whom Jesus says strengthens me in times of peril. It's just that today, when I really, really need comfort and maybe a sign that God is listening, I witness only a gnawing in the pit of my stomach. My head says all the right things, but my heart is shattered. No matter how I try, any formula for getting in touch with God baffles me.

And all the while I plead, "Are you there, God? Hello?"

So I dial and redial, lift my eyes to the sky and hang my head until blood pounds in my ears. My prayer closet is small, cramped, and has no windows. I'm a shipwreck survivor, clinging to the flotsam that's the cross of Christ.

I've learned that no faith resides in comparisons, naming it and claiming it, slogans, or formulae. Maybe those things work for some but not for me, at least not now. I'm no more suited to this solitary phone booth than I ever was, and I still long to collapse into my best friend's arms.

My son may be in chains at this moment, standing before the judge to enter a plea at his arraignment. I pray for God's light to shine through. But judges are human, and only God knows if the truth will be evident today. Injustices are rife in the world; people are starving while others make billions; the whole earth groans. My soul waits for a nudge, a sign, or a crack in heaven's walls. The only comfort I find is in persistence—I must keep calling until Somebody answers. I have to take a chance that the lines to heaven aren't jammed today. It's dangerous to keep on believing in this God whose purposes and actions mystify the human race, yet as Emmanuel Levinas wrote about a story from a Jew in the Warsaw ghetto: "I believe in you, God of Israel, even though you have done everything to stop me from believing in you."[17]

I too cannot stop believing. "My son is in your hands," I say. "Call me back when you get this message."

Fear of Hurting

KRIS: My problem isn't communicating with God. It's the dialogue with other people that scares me. Scares me because I'm so mouthy and I might say something that hurts.

LINDA: Well, I don't think you'd try to hurt someone.

KRIS: Even if I don't try to hurt someone, I can do it inadvertently. And talking to someone very conservative spiritually is scary. I might tread on a toe here or there, or arouse doubt. Be a stumbling block.

LINDA: But do you want to muzzle yourself?

KRIS: No, but I don't always know the best way to talk to someone whom I love and who thinks so differently from me.

A Fundamental Difference

KRIS

Wendy is the best person I know. After twenty years, I've found that she really *is* that sweet, all the way through, really is kind and good to everyone, including her kids, her husband, her dog, and her friends. I don't think she is capable of a bad or vindictive or angry thought. She's generous and invested heavily in the Bible, which she believes contains not only the Word of God but also the words of God.

Say "Word of God" to me and my mind first replies, "Jesus Christ," because he was and is the incarnate Word. Yes, I can say that the Bible is also the Word. If you corner me about the Bible, I'll tell you that I believe in miracles: the parting of the sea, the virgin birth, and the physical resurrection of Jesus. And that whether a worldwide flood actually happened or not, it's a truth within our story. And I believe in evolution, directly God-caused.

Wendy and I are friends, but her fundamentalism and my more scientific theology have built a polite wall between us, a barrier that prevents complete intimacy. Although we both love each other and love the Bible, and both say it's our story, and though we study it

together, we don't say some of the things we think because we fear
hurting each other. I can't tell her about a space telescope's having
glimpsed the beginning of universal time, and when she talks about
the age of the Grand Canyon's being traceable back to the time of
Noah, I think her premise is sincere but scientifically flawed.

How did two Christians get here? When I was a little girl, the
Bible hadn't yet become a polemic that would split—and threaten
to shatter—the church. We didn't know what tolerance was, but we
practiced it. In my small town we were Catholics and Mormons and
many kinds of Protestants (who attended the "community" church
in town). Nowadays all you have to do is watch *Larry King Live* to
see the struggle. When a national tragedy comes about or someone
makes a major religious movie, Larry is sure to interview at least
one Catholic priest and one of several famous evangelicals.

The media are partly responsible. They try to set us at logger-
heads, encouraging us to say we do or don't believe that God made
the world and Jesus saves it; they want a point-by-point argument
over whether the Bible is absolutely inerrant, whether the world is
about ten thousand years old and made in six days, whether God
created Adam from the clay and Eve from his rib, whether Noah
and his family were the only ones saved from the flood, and whether
all known languages originated at the tower of Babel.

Meanwhile, my heart is breaking. My dear friend can't worship
God in the history of the universe, can't permit herself to investigate
string theory or the absolutely divine moment of the Big Bang,
which taught me more about God than anything in the Bible. My
friend is willing to admit that Copernicus was right, that Galileo's
recanting didn't change the position of the earth to the sun, that
denial can't reverse the action of physics; but she can't see the beauty
of the Hubble photographs. I am grieved that she is afraid to listen
to the fact that when an electron pops upward in California, one
pops downward in New York, which should tweak her curiosity,

and the fact of entropy, which says that things tend to become more disordered as they continue, which means that everything in the universe, from rabbits to star clusters, evolved from a place of great order.

And Wendy prays for me because I interpret Scripture and science together. She probably wonders if I have a streak of apostasy that might widen, that I might turn my back on Jesus Christ and, instead, welcome all comers from Buddha to the New Age.

I won't. I'm as firm in my faith in Jesus as my Savior as she is in hers, but our styles are different. I want New Agers to come home to Jesus, and I want literalists to accept those of us with a more metaphorical interpretation of Scripture.

I need to find a way around the wall, not to convince Wendy that I'm right or to admit she's right, but to have a more open relationship, one in which we listen to and accept each other's vision of God. I can't believe that God, with humanlike hands, made Adam out of the clay, but I can believe God had already planned for Adam to be the crown of that creation, had already included all the elements necessary for a garden with a man and woman present.

And then what I need is a way to tell her about it, tell her that I celebrate her beliefs, because they keep me honest and help me as a writer and in ministry. And I hope she will celebrate mine, because I represent a sizable wing of the church, and we need her prayers and respect. And I'll tell her that no matter how old or young we think the world is, God loves us both with such intensity that we both can live in a state of grace forever.

Being an Introvert at Church

LINDA: I'm not just scared of talking to someone whose views differ from mine. I'm enough of an introvert that talking to anyone very long makes me tired. But you showed me how much I was missing by staying away from church.

KRIS: Well, you can be an introvert at church too. I know some people who never shake hands or go to the coffee hour. They just enjoy the service and go home.

LINDA: The faith of the people I meet at church is contagious. It rubs off on me.

KRIS: And there's one thing you can't do alone. Communion is always corporate.

Iron Sharpens Iron

LINDA

She looked at me without judgment or sarcasm. "Why," Kristen asked gently, "don't you have a church home?"

I went into a defensive posture. "I get plenty of God by praying and going on nature walks," I said. "Why, when I lived in Phoenix, I hiked to the top of Squaw Peak every Sunday—at sunup!" I didn't say how emotionally I'd been hurt in my last congregation or that my hikes were mostly for staying in shape or that I liked church well enough, but it was the people I couldn't stand.

I knew the verse in Hebrews against neglecting the assembly, and I never stopped believing. But I admit that I was asking questions and no longer felt comfortable in the nondenominational assembly I'd attended for years. Lately I longed for a certain worship style. The trouble was, I didn't know what that style might be. For me, it took a friendship and a frying pan to make me see my need for community.

Long ago King Solomon declared that two are better than one, and that a three-stranded cord is difficult to break (Eccles. 4:12). During his earthly ministry, Jesus completed the idea by saying, "For where two or three are gathered in my name, I am there among them" (Matt. 18:20). Kristen, God, and I form a triangle of community that I've never doubted.

God shows up, in the backseat of Kristen's little teal green Nissan, tapping a foot along with us as we belt out "De Colores," laughing with us on a wintry afternoon, caressing each of us in our sorrows, playing hide-and-seek in the dappled light through autumn leaves. God isn't the acquaintance we invite when someone cancels at the last minute. He's the guest of honor. And he hones us for the kingdom.

Kristen's and my friendship is like iron sharpening iron. According to that verse, "Iron sharpens iron, and one person sharpens the wits of another" (Prov. 27:17). I picture our bond as a cast-iron skillet. Cast iron makes a great frying pan and it's so versatile—you can cook a delicious omelet or hit a stubborn person over the head with it.

Like a cast-iron frying pan, our friendship has two sides. Once in a while, instead of honing each other, Kristen and I each wield a mean verbal frying pan. Then our friendship is tested.

I'm the first to admit that we're as flawed and human as people come. We love each other, except when we don't. We don't give advice except when we do. Each trusts and confides and is loyal to the extent she is able. As in most relationships, we have ups and downs. Yet because Jesus is among us—and sometimes the referee between us—that cast-iron pan can be used to create a great meal and a lasting peace. My friendship with Kristen is a symbol of the community we all need.

When she asked me about finding a church I liked, I was determined not to have a bad experience again. For a while, I told everyone I was "church shopping," but the truth was that my pride still smarted. I was stuck, spiritually speaking. Rusting away, I saw no need to belong to any community, however welcoming.

But one day the frying pan came down hard on my fears. I don't know exactly what happened, but God got through to me. Go to church, the message came. I'll be there.

God would be there? But what about people—folks who might be like the ones who'd judged me or snubbed me or in some way helped me conclude that fellowship was for fools?

I'll be there. God wouldn't leave me alone. Like Mikey in the old Life cereal commercials, I'd try it.

Which church I chose to try, or even which denomination, isn't important. What matters is that I went to one, and I expected God to sit next to me, to give me the courage to endure being a newcomer, to save my own assessment of this bunch of Christians until I had a chance to get involved.

Guess what? God was there, with bells on. He did sit next to me but reminded me that community isn't all about what you get—that contributing is as important as receiving. Hiking a mountain and calling it church? I couldn't say I'd contributed to much of anything except to the blisters on my feet. Sitting home reading Scripture or praying was good, but it kept me out of touch with others who might need someone to stand with them when things were wrong. Stand with them. Instead of seeing only what I might receive from church, I could cross over to the giving side of God's ways.

As Chuck Swindoll says, "If you hope to make it through days of disillusionment and times of trouble, the secret is friendship. . . . One plus one equals survival."[18] In that little church, I have found smiling faces ready to call me a friend. If this is community, I'll keep coming back for more.

I need to remember that church can be a valuable source of support and encouragement. I'm tempted to isolate myself in times of distress, a tendency I'm trying to change. Yes, I've been wounded, but I want to remember the paralytic who was lowered through the roof, who couldn't have made it to Jesus without a little help from his friends. Instead of saying, "I'd go to church if it wasn't for the people," I'm getting the hang of grace—that everyone's welcome in Jesus's house.

I'm grateful to know Kristen, as well as my friends Jo, Debbie, Kathy, Heather, Melody, and others, because in all our comings and goings, God is there. And as long as God is present, these friendships become community, whether I want them to or not.

That we are friends who love God isn't unusual—many friendships exist among the faithful. What makes these friendships exciting is the web that grows around and through us. By building a spiritual community, God interacts with us through our communion with each other and the holy. We experience God as the Lord outright, in church, study, and worship, and also through exhortation and serendipitous joy.

The more I realize that a whole community praying and comforting me equals God's grace tied with a ribbon, the better I understand the role that my network, friends, and church play in life. The more I'm open to receive direction, assistance, and maybe a simple yet profound prayer when I need it most, the stronger my faith becomes.

Reach out to receive grace in the form of a whole church or simply one close friend, and then stand back. Suddenly the heart senses God standing in the shadows. And for me at least, he doesn't want me to stop at the edges of my comfort zone.

I believe God calls me to reach out to the world, even if it's only through the books I write. As the world shrinks, becoming a "global village," intentional community becomes more important. Diana Butler-Bass writes: "In a broken world God calls the whole of humanity to become God's people."[19] And as sixteenth-century theologian Robert Hooker said, "The Church is called upon to prefigure the kingdom of God."[20]

You may be afraid, as I was, to join a small group at your church, much less be willing to engage in a global community. It's a huge leap from your neighborhood to other cultures. But as prayer and faith unite, as God's people lock arms, the benefits of community emerge: comfort and prayer for each other, strength to do God's mission and work for peace, the invitation that all are welcome in Jesus's house.

What a difference God's presence makes in any relationship! Light shines on hurt raw places that only a friend understands. The stirring of the Holy Spirit evokes tears and joy. A gentle touch delivers "God with skin on" just when it's needed most. When we receive the mystery of the bread and the wine, Jesus reveals himself.

I think God calls Kristen and me to be friends for Christ's sake. But since God hit me over the head with a personal invitation, I've grown into the idea that church is good for me too. I want to get and give the best, and I'm learning to see people through God's eyes. Iron sharpens iron, all right. I hope someday we'll all belong to the community of God's love.

Afraid to Hope

KRIS: Are you ever afraid to hope?

LINDA: Yes. Sometimes I try not to place my hopes too high, so I won't be disappointed. Sort of like jabbing my gums so the dentist won't hurt so much.

KRIS: But could you make yourself stop hoping?

LINDA: I don't think I could stop hoping altogether because Jesus is my hope, the person who says my life matters.

KRIS: What Jesus has been showing me is that my life may not matter so much, that the world won't be worse off when I die. He's showing me how to put my hope into heaven.

LINDA: [pants, sighs, moans] I have a hard time with heaven by and by.

KRIS: Well, you will have hope in heaven as you age. And you want to be fit for it because you could leave here today and get hit by a truck.

LINDA: Well, I know I'm fit for heaven, because Someone says I am. Whosoever believeth . . .

KRIS: If we hope for heaven, then what is the "hope laid up for you in heaven" that Paul talks about? Does that mean heaven is hoping for me to make it or that when I get to heaven, I still have to hope? Sometimes hope can be dangerous.

LINDA: Earthly hope is the most dangerous. If I hope for a nice Thanksgiving meal, and Uncle Charlie shows up drunk, I will be disappointed. And disappointment is hard.

WORKING IT OUT

Wrestling with Living Like We Believe

When God Gets Mad

LINDA: Do you ever think God's mad at you?

KRIS: Once. About thirty or more years ago. A woman made overtures of friendship to me, and I sidestepped her. I'd seen the police at their house, and I knew she had problems. I was struggling with my own neuroses, but one morning I saw them carry her out, dead, in a rubber sheet. Maybe I couldn't have saved her life, but I could have at least had coffee with her. God didn't talk to me for about three weeks. He never scolded or threatened me. He was absolutely silent. Let me tell you, I'll never ignore another person who's clutching the hem of my garment.

LINDA: Man. Just admitting that took a lot of courage, didn't it?

KRIS: I went back to that time and remembered my guilty tears.

LINDA: Imagine what life would be like if we thought God was mad at us all the time. If I thought that, I would only be afraid of God. Loving God wouldn't be easy. Yet these days I sense God straining to reach through the ether to touch me. There's a desperation on God's part that I never noticed before.

KRIS: One of the ways I like to describe my life with God is that I feel welcomed. God makes me an honored guest.

LINDA: I can hardly remember my life without Jesus Christ.

157

With Fear and Trembling

LINDA

In March of 1979 I waited by the window for a couple to pick me up for a spiritual service. My firstborn son, Nathaniel Micah, nestled against my chest, wrapped snugly in a cloth baby carrier, because he was so colicky. I was a new mom, nervous and unsure about nearly everything. I worried that my ride wouldn't show up, and while I waited, I watched a trail of ants on the bougainvillea just outside the window.

The ants were hauling in a huge catch—a live moth passed jaw over jaw along the ant trail. They handled their prey in communal fashion, pulling together as one. Every member seemed to sense responsibility to the group, and in turn, individuals received membership, sustenance, and purpose. I don't know where the hill and queen lay, but I got swept up in the drama. I became the moth, in the mandibles of the enemy, bumping along to its fate.

The farthest point I could see was at the edge of the roof, where the ants would need to form a living chain or leap across a half-inch-wide space between the bush and the house. If those worker ants were marching to their own deaths, they didn't know it. Nathan made suckling noises and I swayed side to side, rocking him. Then he was quiet again. The moth wings fluttered and stilled.

I stood on the brink of my life and wondered if I was dead or alive. I had an infant son, sure, but I didn't know if anything in the world was really solid, with laws and rules I could count on to be the same every day. What if the sun forgot to rise tomorrow? I wasn't even certain who or what lay behind the design of a trillion insects or the precise curvature of the planet. My kid sister, Leslie, had always insisted God was what I needed, along with salvation, a good Bible, and maybe an exorcism.

But Leslie was far away. The moth's movements looked weaker. My chest heaved with a soundless sigh, and the baby stirred. I walked back and forth, keeping one eye on the ants as well as the street in case my ride showed up after all. These acquaintances tended toward tardiness, but tonight they were downright flakes.

I'd joined the metaphysical group to rid myself of my angry childhood God, who stalked me wherever I went. I met my husband in Southern California and moved four hundred miles to start a new life with him. For a few months, God backed off and I jogged the beaches, trying to raise my consciousness and lose ten pounds.

My only support group was metaphysical not Christian. Our particular cult was a blend of Christianity, Science of Mind, and the occult. Everybody loved Jesus and a pantheon of inner Christs. The women gave child-rearing advice as well as tarot card readings. One older lady offered to babysit my son while she worked out someone's astrological chart. Most of them were so ordinary, if you didn't know they were commanding tables to move on their own, you'd think they were nice Christians.

Before you swoon, I was raised and baptized as a Protestant. I wandered into the occult the same way I'd wandered into my life, the same way the ants meandered up the bougainvillea. They didn't stop until they came to the end of the flaming magenta flowers. I never thought I'd need a reason to keep living until I came to my personal jumping-off place.

But when I gave birth at age twenty-seven, I panicked. I wanted a life I could count on. Lately I'd noticed most of the people in the New Age group were down-and-out. No one seemed to be prospering the way they visualized, including my husband and me.

He'd resumed drinking, perhaps to cope with the stress, and our marriage was failing. My little boy and I lived in a strange town and I had no car, few friends, no one to help me. If I were the moth, would I leap from the bougainvillea into the air? Would I demand to speak to the God who made leaping possible?

Needless to say, I was depressed. Dabbling with occult practices made me feel guilty and prone to nightmares. Like Annie Dillard's moth, though, I couldn't stop myself from playing with fire. (Annie Dillard has compared the writing life to that of a moth—inexplicably bound to fly into a flame, burned by its truth and beauty.) I flirted with the idea of a godless universe, a place full of reflex and instinct, gravity, and cause and effect. All the occult claims of astral travel, past lives, and future predictions promised I'd find the Answer. All I'd found were thinly disguised lies and a reeking diaper pail.

Since Nathan's birth, my days and nights staggered through an endless cycle of infant care: diaper, nursing, burping, nap, nursing, walking, bath, and diapers in between. Rash, screaming through dinner, nursing, walking, walking, walking. The daddy was so overwhelmed that he sometimes didn't bother to come home until after the bars closed. I was so postpartum bluesy, a million ants could tap-dance on cue and I wouldn't laugh.

Maybe this was a headless universe, just going through the motions, uninterested in moths and humans alike.

I watched the ant trail, and suddenly nothing made sense. My son was two months old—he wasn't predictable about anything.

The couple that offered me a ride was late. My husband wasn't home. Again.

I craned my neck to see the end of the line for those ants. Sure enough, one brave worker hung by its back legs, front end flailing, antennae going crazy. He poised on the edge of the bush while a thousand of his brothers bottlenecked into gridlock. The moth was stuck in traffic.

If I were a moth going to slaughter, I guess I'd be thanking the stars for any delay. Even a short reprieve might help me get my eggs laid so I could die in peace. Peace. A chord played somewhere and I choked on my own surprise.

Oh! I needed the comfort of something I dimly remembered—Jesus, always there, always loving. My heart ached for a God who'd conquered death and who, some said, was keenly interested in the world. Ants, moths, and tipsy husbands, this God welcomed them all.

Ageless Jesus beckoned to a frantic, tired new mother, nipples still raw. The Creator of this perfect, cranky baby had watched his mommy as she hauled him to church, loaded him in a fold-up stroller, and folded him across her arm like a dishtowel when he cried and cried. In between creation and lunch, Jesus hadn't taken his eyes off me.

I knew what I had to do.

Nathan bleated out a small cry and my milk let down all at once. Tears I had stored for months tumbled out because only Jesus can do that to me. One look, one touch from Christ and I'm reduced to blubbering like a baby. In a sacred instant, he swept away the false and ladled out a generous portion of love. My knees weakened and I didn't know if I could survive another dose of the holy. God blazed in the bougainvillea and I had to turn my face away.

I called my kid sister the instant I could, and she led me through the sinner's prayer. The metaphysics group? Well, I'd let them know

I was dropping out when I got time. I'd tell them I served the one true God now, and that Jesus is, for me anyway, the only Answer. On a newborn faith in Jesus Christ as Lord and Savior, I shot into the unknown on the promise of eternal life.

I was glad no one came to fetch me that evening, because now my shirt was wet with milk. I settled into my nursing chair and lifted Nathan out of his carrier. He took to suckling in his usual robust way, with loud smacks and delighted grunts. When I looked back outside, the moth was gone.

In God's Presence

LINDA: I remember how scared I was to invite Jesus into my life.

KRIS: What were you the most scared of?

LINDA: What scared me most was that I thought I'd have to give up everything that didn't have a direct connection to God. I could only do art that depicted religious scenes; I could only read the Bible and listen to gospel music.

KRIS: And how long did you live that way, running scared?

LINDA: At least ten years. I raised my kids on *Christian Mother Goose* and James Dobson.

KRIS: And you couldn't go to movies or listen to other music?

LINDA: I lost the eighties. I didn't know who the rock stars were or what movies were popular or even what books were on the best-seller list. And then one day, I realized my kids hadn't benefited from going without Nintendo.

KRIS: How about now?

LINDA: At last I'm experiencing a spiritual life in which the people around me infuse me with their joy and excitement for God and for one another. Do you get the feeling that you're in a great crowd of people who pull you up and into God's presence?

KRIS: Yeah. It's called the Church Triumphant. The church in heaven and the church on earth are connected. There's no division between them, in God's eyes, no matter how we quarrel over the form of baptism or the date of Easter.

Cloud of Witnesses

KRIS

Therefore, since we are surrounded by so great a cloud of witnesses,
let us also lay aside every weight and the sin that clings so closely,
and let us run with perseverance the race that is set before us.

Hebrews 12:1

In the 1920s a devout woman named Lesbia Scott wrote hymns
for her children. One was for All Saints' Day, November 1, and it
speaks of not only that cloud of witnesses that have departed this
life but those who are everywhere on earth. The first verse says:

I sing a song of the saints of God,
Patient and brave and true,
Who toiled and fought and lived and died
For the Lord they loved and knew.
And one was a doctor,
And one was a queen,
And one was a shepherdess on the green:
They were all of them saints of God—and I mean,
God helping, to be one too.

In 2002, a week past All Saints' Day, I stood in a churchyard
while the November wind tossed orange and red leaves against my

boots and past the tombstone of my great-great-great-great-great-grandfather, John Johnson. And I sang "The Saints of God" aloud as I stood there, loving my ancestors and their place in the Cloud of Witnesses.

John came to southern New Jersey in 1756 with his wife, Jane, so he could freely exercise his strict, almost ascetic Presbyterian faith. His grave bears a DAR plaque and an American flag, because besides being a Presbyterian, he was a Revolutionary patriot, a New Jersey Minuteman.

I can't let him down.

And all around his headstone lie the graves where some of my foreparents are buried. One hundred early Americans sleep in the Old Pittsgrove Presbyterian churchyard, built in 1741 in Daretown, New Jersey—and I am related to seventy of that hundred. On the other side of my family, I have Scots who fled first to Ireland and then to America, because they too were Presbyterians. My lines include Mayflower Puritans who escaped from England and came here to worship and embattled Quakers from Wales; many were Huguenots from France or Flanders, and some Anglican clergy who fled from the persecution of Mary Tudor.

And I can't let them down.

And if Levi paid his tithes while he was in the loins of Abraham, paid them to Melchizedek a thousand years before Levi was born, then my ancestors worshiped for me when I was two hundred or more years yet unborn. They came here and scrabbled in the American dirt to build Protestant churches with tall white spires or quiet Quaker meetinghouses or stone Dutch Reformed churches on the green. We may not think of this country as holy, especially nowadays; but to a man or woman escaping religious persecution, America was God's country and walking on its soil became a spiritual exercise.

I believe this Cloud of Witnesses still prays for me: Standing in front of God's throne, they pray for my edification and knowledge and—since some of them were very strict Calvinists—that I be predestinated for salvation. Keep praying that prayer, dear ancestors. Just in case.

And I can't let any of them down. They're waiting, and I have a duty to them: to live up to their prayers, to reverence their difficult lives as American colonials who had to fight a war with their homeland so they could keep being Calvinists and Quakers and Episcopalians. When I found out that my ancestral grandmother was injured during the Revolution when she ran messages from George Washington to patriots behind enemy lines, I realized what the fight for freedom of religion meant to her descendants. One Huguenot ancestor was "erased by Inquisitors," according to the record, before he could get on ship. And another fell ill and was unable to debark. He asked to be propped up on deck where he could look at Boston Harbor, the "promised land," as he called it, the place where he could be a Protestant. He died there.

And since I have this heritage, this cloud of physical and spiritual ancestors, I have to run with perseverance the race set before me. I have to "lay aside every weight and the sin that clings so closely." There are days when I indeed wish I could lay aside every weight, especially that in the middle of my body, but the writer of Hebrews was of course speaking of sin and distraction and anything else that burdens us. Lay it aside, the verse means, and take Christ's easy burden instead.

Paul addressed many of his letters to the saints in various cities. Sometimes it was to those "called to be saints." Am I so called? Are you? Was Mother Teresa? Of course, the answers lie in your definition of a saint. In Paul's world the church hadn't started canonizing the holiest of the departed, and "saint" meant a person consecrated to God, or a Christian, one of God's beloved. And we should celebrate that state in ourselves, because we are connected spiritually to the Cloud that surrounds us. I'm connected not only to my bloodline ancestors, but to every person who left this world in a state of grace and to our brothers and sisters on earth:

They loved their Lord so dear, so dear,
And his love made them strong;
And they followed the right, for Jesus' sake,
The whole of their good lives long.
And one was a soldier,
And one was a priest,
And one was slain by a fierce wild beast:
And there's not any reason—no, not the least,
Why I shouldn't be one too.

When my father died, I asked to have the words of 2 Timothy 4:7 read at his memorial service: "I have fought the good fight, I have finished the race, I have kept the faith."

The young pastor looked up, surprised, when I made my request. "Do you mean this?" he asked. "Is this really about your father?" When I said yes, tears sprang to his eyes. "I have a daughter," he said. "I wonder if she can say this about me when I die."

And I wonder if my children or grandchildren will be able to say, "She ran the race" or "She kept the faith." And moreover, I can only hope that my Cloud of Witnesses will welcome me as one who fought the good fight, one who was called to be a saint.

They lived not only in ages past,
There are hundreds of thousands still,
The world is bright with the joyous saints
Who love to do Jesus' will.
You can meet them in school, or
In lanes, or at sea,
In church, or in trains, or in shops, or at tea,
For the saints of God are just folk like me,
And I mean to be one too.[21]

Who's That God I Saw You With?

KRIS: All I can say is, if God is a figment of my imagination, why isn't God the one I would invent?

LINDA: Then there would have to be six billion versions of God because everyone would have a different idea. What astonishes me is that all the major religions of the world have a God who's the creator, has rules, and provides some way to get to eternal bliss. So which one's right?

KRIS: All of them have some basic truth, but they may not contain the kind of grace Jesus offers us. Christianity isn't a doctrine; it's a Person.

LINDA: I admit that I ask a lot of questions. But when I ask God to show me the truth, I get Jesus. And even if I try to change my mind, Jesus pursues me. At my lowest points, when I was sure God had abandoned me, Jesus was there. And he'd been there all the time.

KRIS: And when you look back at your life, you see that he was present, even when you thought you were in hell.

LINDA: How can we open our lives more completely to Jesus and still find time for work and play?

KRIS: I don't try.

Balancing Act

KRIS

Too often people ask, "How do you balance your life with writing and family and church and everything?"

I've listened to the ways others said they managed: quiet time with God every day, dinner always with family or friends, walks outdoors or on a treadmill, writing about three hours a day, or—for those married—setting aside romantic time with the spouse.

What a crock.

I make no attempt to live a balanced life.

If you're really working for God, even the best schedules and plans will go out the window or down the drain or into the trash. I make no effort to lead such an ordered life, because God has no sense of balance. What God wants is everything, and wants it right now.

Here's the situation. You're carrying your spouse, your kids, the groceries, and your job on your left arm and hip; on the right side, you're holding a six-foot cross over your shoulder. Sometimes you drop some groceries or let your job roll down the driveway, and other times, you fall down on your right side, cross and all. You can get up and balance for maybe a minute at a time, and then you crash again.

Eventually, you'll realize you may have to put something down so you can get both arms around the cross.

What? Put more care into carrying the cross than in your family or work? Well, Jesus did say, "Whoever loves father or mother more than me is not worthy of me; and whoever loves son or daughter more than me is not worthy of me; and whoever does not take up the cross and follow me is not worthy of me."

Uh-huh. That's one of those verses we try to get around, try to rearrange. Scripture contains a number of them, but you rarely hear any of them preached about or studied. And when we do discuss them, we say, "Well, of course what Jesus really meant is that we should follow him by being good parents, or good sons and daughters, or good computer programmers."

But deep down, we know. We know what he's asking. The word is *miseo*, hate or discard. If your grandson has leukemia, and you lose your faith over it, you have loved your child or parent more than Jesus Christ. No matter what happens to anyone, you're supposed to keep pure your love for Jesus. I wonder if I would survive if one of my children or grandsons died. I imagine a world without my kids and grandkids in it and I reel backwards, fall into terrifying mystery, drop through a thousand miles of darkness, plunge onto the hot, hard rock at the center of the earth. I would try to brush away my images of Jesus, try to stop my ears from hearing his words. I might even scream, "I hate you, Jesus," as I fell, but I couldn't really bring myself to think I didn't love him anymore.

So I clamber up and shoulder my cross again. And I always think there's a way to get this right; that all I have to do is find it. At the beginning of this book I quoted Rowan Williams, who said God always has to be rediscovered, meaning that God always has to be heard or seen where there aren't yet words for him. So I look and listen, not only at beautiful sunsets or children's voices, but into the face of a starving woman in Sudan or a hurricane-destroyed mobile home, or hear the shouts of the police at a disgusting landfill where a man tossed his dead wife. Why does God permit this? Somehow the answer lies in our surrender to carrying the cross.

And surrender to God is the answer, as hard as that is for me to say. Once I listened to a radio evangelist who was alternately preaching and laying on hands for healing. When he touched one woman, sounds told me she fell down, unable to move or speak. There was a shuffling sound as if people were coming to help her, but the preacher's voice boomed, "Leave her lay! Leave her lay where the Lord flang her!"

Because this was radio, I couldn't tell whether the evangelist pushed her or she fell. I don't know what she said when she woke up, or whether she had an honest-to-God spiritual experience. Whatever you think about being "slain in the Spirit," a great truth, maybe the great truth, dances through the preacher's words: when God flings us somewhere, we better stay put.

However, God doesn't want us to be victims, because we have one Victim already, one who can live your life and die your death. And even teach you love. Not just that wonderful first love that we talked about a few chapters ago, but grown-up love, the kind that's meant to last.

When I was just married, we lived in a shabby housekeeping apartment, madly in love. Looking back, I can see why my mother was anxious about my being in that part of town, but at the time I thought our apartment and the streetcar I rode to work were wonderful. We were delighted with each other; we had small dinner parties where I served the salad in a cooking pot and everyone got one piece of chicken. We sat on the floor, we played charades and listened to Shostakovich's Sixth on our fourth-hand record player. Love colored the drab walls and turned the drippy icebox and rickety stove into shiny appliances. We had everything we needed: each other. When trouble came along, we fought it together, and usually won. If we could have made those days last forever we might have changed the world. We weren't living a balanced life, because when we weren't at work or cooking, we were making love.

It should have lasted forever, but because we were both so human, love wore away like stone does under running water. But when one of you is God, glorious love can last forever. Only the love of Christ can lift us out of our earthly confusion and teach us how to live, without balance but with the richest thing the universe offers us: God.

Jesus Christ lives an unbalanced life, too, because his love for the Church is what he cares about most. For us became a man—something C. S. Lewis compared to our becoming a slug or a crab. Jesus opened his arms to any who would come. He was betrayed and made to suffer. He died a criminal's death. He harrowed hell and released the prisoners there. He rose from the dead and ascended into heaven and will come back for us. And none of this, none of this was because we were good or balanced or even had good sense, because we weren't and aren't and don't.

Yes, while we live on earth, we'll have trouble. People we love— even little babies—get sick and die. Evil walks over the earth in broad daylight. Murderers and rapists get out of jail and repeat their crimes. Young people buy drugs from other young people who are supporting their habits. The mentally ill are spilled out into the streets where they are abused or killed by others, or cause problems for ordinary people. The suicide rate is rampant. The economy is unstable, wars go on and on, husbands murder their wives, and women drown their children. Earth is a bad place and has been since the first moment someone wanted power or coveted his neighbor's house or car or wife. So what if you're living in abject poverty or got fired from your job or one of your children has an attachment disorder or your mother is dying? What if the only thing you have is misery?

It never is. You may have misery, but you also always have Jesus, coaxing you, pleading with you, daring you to cast all your cares on him because you matter to him. If you don't hear him or feel his presence, call him. Ask him not only to live in your heart, but to let you live in his.

Scared? Good. God is dangerous, and if you are in God, you'll get burned. Burned alive. Melted down until your spirit is the pure gold that God made it to be. And by then you will have forgotten all about balance.

These Holy Mysteries

LINDA: What a relief to give up juggling! But before I allow God to burn me, I must decide to believe. Our pastor said in a sermon that one of the reasons he believes is because he was taught, discipled at an early age. But somewhere, he had to take the leap of faith himself, didn't he?

KRIS: I never know how much of my faith was learned, how much was a gift from God, and how much I grasped on my own. But the God I live with isn't like the one I'd invent. I think I want Santa Claus with a degree in philosophy. That's what I meant at the beginning. If, as atheists say, God is an invention of the mind, then God should act the way I want, not only offering me grace and benevolence but also money and fame or something.

LINDA: Unfortunately, even my version of Santa Claus includes strict rules about behavior, a lump of coal in my stocking, and the terror that he judges me as naughty or nice, usually naughty. My ideal God would love everything I do, think I'm the best, and make things turn out okay.

KRIS: Well, you do have a God who loves everything you do and thinks you're the best. The turning-out-okay thing is the problem.

LINDA: You're right. So right. But I look around, and there Jesus is, again. The turning-out-okay part is connected to whether God is fair.

KRIS: God isn't fair; God is just. There's a difference.

LINDA: I see that difference more and more in my life. At church I see people sacrificing to build homes for the homeless, feed the hungry, and bring good clothes for the poor. At McDonald's, I see people offering to buy lunch for those in need. Aren't those examples of God's justice?

KRIS: Then are we God's instruments of justice?

LINDA: Well, who else is going to do it? Not too many loaves and fishes getting multiplied at picnics here.

KRIS: In the Bible, justice has nothing to do with law enforcement or people getting punished. Bible justice is what we call charity—justice for the poor, the widowed, the homeless.

LINDA: So that God I saw you with doesn't sound like anyone either of us would invent. This God loves us whether we deserve it or not, sacrificed himself for the life of the world, and is alive, here, today. Christ has died; Christ is risen; Christ will come again.

KRIS: I'm afraid that no matter how many flimsy little Santa gods we could invent, the real One is more irresistible. I could love my invention until I looked up and saw the real thing. Or Person, as it were.

LINDA: You can't ignore Jesus. And that's what makes Christianity so dangerous.

7

THE BIG PICTURE

Wrestling with Power

Storm Chasers

KRIS: Well, we've loved God, fought with God, even doubted God; but here we are, a pair of believers, surrendering to that same God.

LINDA: I'm not the person I was when we started.

KRIS: And neither is God, or at least, neither is our perception of God.

LINDA: Do you think God changes?

KRIS: I think God is a continuing revelation.

LINDA: God is a lot bigger now than he was a couple of years ago. And his mystery is greater but not so scary.

KRIS: God's size is immeasurable, inestimable. And I might add, "immortal, invisible, God only wise" like the epistle to Timothy, and the hymn.[22] Just singing that hymn makes God immense in my mind.

LINDA: Let's chase God!

KRIS: I think I hear him saying, "You ain't seen nothing yet."

The Wizard on the Screen

KRIS

I always love the moment in the movie *The Wizard of Oz* when Dorothy's little dog, Toto, yanks the curtain and reveals that the terrifying Oz on the screen is just electric plasma; the real "wizard" is a clever white-haired snake-oil purveyor who hides behind the curtain and works the mechanical illusion.

The Great Oz didn't exist, even in that magical kingdom where bad witches gazed into crystal balls, monkeys flew, scarecrows walked and talked, and lions were easily frightened. Oz was a fake, as phony as the patent medicines the "wizard" had peddled in the black-and-white world.

Atheists and other religious detractors point to that movie scene to suggest that there's no God who can heal the sick and the blind, and they make fun of a God who, they say, is in charge of everything from football games to wars. Show us proof, they say. Like Herod in *Jesus Christ Superstar*, they ask Jesus to walk across swimming pools, and they laugh at our belief in an invisible God. They say Christians are at best deluded and at worst charlatans who proclaim a big, powerful God, but that little wizards—priests or pastors, theologians, and Christian writers—are behind the curtain, manipulating the vision.

But the reverse is true. I don't know why the God we tell people about and write books about is too often a narrow-minded, angry little magician, a carnival barker who punishes sinners and occasionally waves a wand, while he hides the real God who is behind the draperies: an immense and powerful God, whose concealing curtain is the whole universe.

And those who deny God are made even angrier because we can't give them a decent description of the one we worship. They may not realize that the minute someone suggests what God is like, they've limited and put boundaries on God. In fact, even the statement, "God is too mysterious to know" is a definition and therefore shrunken and constricted.

Atheists notwithstanding, I wonder if anyone can know what and who God is or predict God's behavior or understand God's will. Sure, we can demonstrate God's intention through the Bible, but not all the studies in the world will really tell us what God wants from us and from the spinning galaxies and the tiniest microbe.

Once at a church potluck, I asked the particle physicist who sings in our choir about whether neutron stars emitted any light. We talked for a few minutes about string theories and the news that, despite Einstein's theories, light is not a constant in quasars, and then he said in his soft voice, "Everything we know about physics is an anomaly. We only know the exceptions not the rules."

That idea was so overwhelming that I nearly fainted. I pushed my plate away and sucked in my breath, not only because he turned my understanding of physical science and astronomy on its head, but because his declaration went to the heart of Christian theology. The sacrifice and resurrection of Jesus Christ were anomalies. Every miracle is an exception; every act of love or sacrifice is outside the rule.

And the rule? Only God knows. Physicists search matter, astronomers sled from galaxy to galaxy, biologists comb our genes, archaeologists dig through our pasts, and they're all looking for a theory of everything. They brush together now and then: Mathematicians seek answers in music; botanists study desire; and according to at least one journalist, physicists dance their way into knowledge. Gary Zukav, a science writer, says that most people believe that physicists are explaining the world and that some physicists even believe that; but he believes they are dancing with it, trying to engage not what they already know, but what they can imagine and hope for.

Does this mean that reality as we know it is an illusion? Philosophers as far back as Plato and as recent as Sartre investigated the idea that what we see and touch doesn't exist if we are not here to observe it, or that all we know are reflections on the backs of cave walls of absolute universals. Heady stuff, but what do they have to do with God?

I think everything we know, not just the laws of physics, was transformed into something different, into a new reality, poured into the stream of experience as an anomaly, when Christ touched down on earth. The human condition could then become something beyond the rules, could break free and soar because we are immortal beings who race madly toward the throne of God so we can get on with eternity.

Is God scary? Yes, indeed. But Jesus Christ stands in front of you at the throne, whispering to his Father, "No condemnation." That's how important you are: that God became a man for your sake and then pulls you into heaven on his shirttails, or shawl tassels, as it were. So, like the subatomic world that won't conform to Newton's laws, the God who occupies perhaps a million universes pours into the person of Christ, and we have to have a quantum theory to explain him.

We only catch glimpses of the great Being. We saw him on earth as Jesus Christ, who might be called a hologram of God. If you drop a hologram, every single shattered piece contains the whole picture; and Christ's shattered body and blood, shed on the soil in Israel two thousand years ago, left the picture and the presence of God throughout the earth.

We also see if not God, then God's handiwork in every fir tree and columbine and baby lamb. We gasp when we behold his work in the Hubble Space Telescope photographs. We hear God speak in waterfalls and in lightning, through the Bible and whispering into our prayers. And we feel God's presence in worship, as we sing or kneel or lift our hands, and we hear God's majesty when the organ booms "A Mighty Fortress Is Our God" or when the toddlers' choir sings "This Little Light of Mine." And that certainly isn't all. What we know about God wouldn't fill a spiritual thimble. Anyone who reads the Bible daily, thinking that all of God is contained in the Word, hasn't looked behind the curtain. Or at the stars. Or into the depths of the sea.

Which brings me back to the choice between the wizard of Oz or the universal God who is boiling and dancing behind the immense curtain. Some of my more shallow prayers are probably directed to the little snake-oil salesman, the carnival barker. But my deeper prayers, the devotions that fling me out to dance among the stars, the prayers to El Shaddai, make me want to tear the great veil away, rip it off with my hands, and expose myself to the real God, whose radiation could turn me into a black print on the sidewalk or reveal a love that occupies every molecule of the universe.

Why keep living, even when life is hard? Because the Son of God dances in the meadow. The figs are ripe, and God says, live. Live.

Which is what all this is about. In the beginning, God created heaven and earth, whether God created the earth in six literal days or Big-Banged the universe together with a word. The Word, God's name, means something like "I Live." Don't watch the little wizard, who can only nod and smile. Instead, look through Newton and Einstein, peer past quantum mechanics and strings and the special theory of relativity. Throw yourself at the heart of God, and when you get there, you can finally whisper an authentic, "Please?"

The Dance of God

LINDA: Whoa! Wu Li masters and the new physics?[23]

KRIS: You don't have to be a physicist to understand the universe as a dance—the dance of God. In the last chapter of C. S. Lewis's *Peralandra*, he describes the Great Dance with no reference to physics.

LINDA: But it excites me on to know that the constant movement of physical particles, electrons, neutrons, quarks, even in solid things like tables and stones, is a dance.

KRIS: Maybe an angelic dance around the throne?

LINDA: I wonder if God dances too. Or maybe God is the music. So our faith is a matter of dancing the Word?

KRIS: Spoken like a Wu Li master.

LINDA: A master fighting for faith.

Fighting for Faith

LINDA

Grandma Gypsy's prayers could peel the paint off a wall. She was also the most spiritual person I knew—a devout Southern Baptist who talked openly about Jesus, prayed a lot, and read her *Guiding Light* devotions every morning. I met her when I was nine, after she and my grandfather moved out west from Pennsylvania. In a short time I wanted what I thought she had. I was desperate for God.

Nobody at my house talked much about spiritual things. For a time, when we lived in Yuma, Arizona, my mother had played the piano for the Methodist church. During that period, I attended Sunday school—we made tents for the twelve tribes of Israel, using fabric scraps, toothpicks, and pieces of salt dough. I thought the activity was meaningless busywork and longed to find the true God—whom, I imagined, lived in the Big Church. At home I pretended to lead Big Church and sang hymns, hoping I could get as big a faith as Grandma had.

Then our family moved to Phoenix. Mom worked full-time and no longer played hymns on Sunday morning. By then our family journeyed to church once a year on Easter, like a pilgrimage. The rest of the time my father and mother's faith hid behind the American dream. On bright Arizona weekends, Mom and Dad and my little sister, Leslie, dressed in swimsuits and did yard work, while I stayed indoors due to my severe allergies. I still longed to find God, so once again I turned to Grandmother Gypsy for spiritual direction.

One year she presented me with a white leather-bound Bible, complete with zipper and my name stamped in gold on the front. This Bible was the King James Red Letter Version, which meant all the words Jesus spoke were printed in red. The white Bible was my prize possession, and on my long hospital stays for orthopedic surgeries, I kept it under my pillow like a talisman. At home I toted it everywhere. I tried to memorize verses, joined a Sunday school Bible club, and attended summer church camp.

Every week I went to church with Grandma Gypsy. Grandpa was our chauffeur because my grandmother had never learned to drive. Every week we lumbered into the gravel parking lot in his ancient Chevrolet, a roundish sedan, hand-painted in kelly green. I knew it had been hand-painted from the brush marks. Every week Grandpa sat outside in the green car because he was a Methodist and refused to set foot in the Baptist church.

In a way, I didn't blame him. Grandma's preacher was of the hellfire variety, and his sermons shook any nappers out of their repose. On one hot summer Sunday, I begged to attend Big Church—Sunday school was for babies. God surely attended the grown-up service.

We filed in and took our seats—I can't remember if they were pews or folding chairs. While we droned out a hymn (it really was too hot to sing), I looked around. The room was plain, save for an enormous cross behind the pulpit and an organ to one side. Dull brown carpet marked the aisle. Grandma Gypsy gave me a pen to doodle on the bulletin, but I told her, "I won't need to draw. I'm too old for that."

Then the preacher banged his palm against the podium, and I snapped to attention. Behind him the giant cross towered up toward the A-frame roof. "The wages of sin is death!" he bellowed from the pulpit. "You must die to sin!"

I flinched. I wished I could put my hands over my ears, but that would be bad manners. Instead, I let my favorite *Hit Parade* song, "The Lion Sleeps Tonight," run through my mind. I drew a lion in one corner of the paper, with a gaping jaw full of teeth.

Grandma, sitting next to me in her Sunday dress and a brown cloche with a little net hanging in front like bangs, didn't appear to mind the preacher's barrage. Knees politely together, her hands folded on her lap, she didn't seem surprised at the directive.

The sermon made my eyes sting. I thought, *So this is the grown-up God.* Maybe you had to be scared to be saved. Maybe in order to get close to God, you had to get your soul blasted clean. If Jesus loved me and wanted me to live forever, why did the preacher keep shouting about death?

The preacher took a deep breath and then jabbed his index finger at the congregation, while holding his Bible draped across his other hand. "For he who has died is freed from sin." He pointed again, this time up at the cross in back of him. "Surrender! Crucify your will at the foot of the cross! You can't get to Jesus any other way!"

I was terrified of the yelling and because crucifixion sounded really painful. I sat as far back against the seat as I could. I couldn't let Grandma know I was not grown-up enough for Big Church. I couldn't let her know how scary this version of God seemed to a nine-year-old. After that day, I went back to the Sunday school, where Jesus had lambs and invited children to sit on his lap, and where the Almighty seemed more like Santa Claus, one where a pleasing sacrifice often involved glue, construction paper, and glitter. I had to find God somewhere.

As I got older, my search intensified. I joined a church choir. My folks came to see me sing, which made me feel as if my family finally had a faith. But I was chronically ill with bronchitis, so I missed a lot of choir performances. Times when I was too sick to sit in the choir loft, I sat in the pew and sucked furiously on lifesavers so I wouldn't cough so hard during the sermon.

This minister was Grandma's preacher's opposite. The reverend told *Peanuts* jokes and spoke in a soft voice. He had a wide, easy grin and was very kind. But the sixties had hit, and I was swept up with ideals about peace and love and a boyfriend who smoked pot and wore his hair long.

When we decided to get married, my folks insisted I get pre-marital counseling with my hippie husband-to-be. My fiancé and I sat before the kind minister, who shook his head in disbelief at our lack of preparation for marriage. He married us, but I think he could see our union wouldn't last.

My traditional upbringing collided with the social upheaval of the era. I decided the Protestant God I'd searched so hard to find now disapproved of my lifestyle. The church and I had nothing more to say to each other.

I said I dropped out of the choir to find God, but I really was in search of myself. I experimented with metaphysics, Eastern thought, and the occult, which grieved my family and my poor grandmother. After a while, the marriage failed, as I expect the minister had predicted. I spent several years teaching school, and countless lonely nights, desperate for meaning, certain that God was out there somewhere. But where?

Finally, I landed in Southern California, where the New Age movement seemed a logical continuation of peace and love. On the beach I sought belonging with a new sort of people who worshiped Jesus and a host of other inner gods. I tried to fix my faith by moving to San Diego. I met a man, married again, and finally, at twenty-seven, had a son.

Only something was wrong. Not only did my new husband have problems with alcohol, I chafed at the notion of a bunch of inner gods solving my problems. While Science of Mind practitioners taught me meditation and visualization to improve my life, I saw only a sad-faced Jesus, standing in the corner of my mind. When the cult I had joined put on a Christmas Pageant, I welcomed the chance to sing again. But during choral practice, I learned this pageant honored the birth of Jesus not as God Incarnate, crucified, and resurrected, but as one of many deities deserving attention. I felt more cut off from God than ever. So instead of going home that chilly December evening, I went to the beach.

I walked near the water's edge and then climbed up a steep path to the top of a cliff overlooking the Pacific Ocean. I stood at sunset, desperate as always. I had to decide whether to stay in La Jolla or take my infant son and return to my home in Arizona. I prayed as hard as I ever have.

The light was fading; the sun edged toward a deep blue horizon. In a few minutes I'd be swallowed by darkness—the darkness of circumstances and my own folly.

Spray from the crashing waves salted my face. Pebbles skittered down the sheer cliff face, a reminder of the avalanche of my life. Finally, I screamed out, "God, if you're there, give me a sign!"

The wind hurtled my voice back at me. I closed my eyes and I felt as if a cloak surrounded me, so dark I couldn't see. When I opened my eyes the sun was gone. I still had no idea what God wanted me to do, and I felt very alone. In the dark, the path to the parking lot disappeared into the mist.

In my mind I saw Grandma's twinkly blue eyes, sure of what she believed. I had to remember how attracted I'd been to her strength, how in good times and bad she always relied on Jesus. Her Jesus was not only a lamb-toting Good Shepherd or simply one of many gods. For Grandma Gypsy, Jesus was everything. She had somehow accepted the lamb and lion sides of the same Jesus. Her faith was nothing, she'd always say, but leaning on the Lord. Her method seemed simple and perilous to me. More than ever, I needed what she had.

Try not to melt in your contact with me, the wind said. Don't run. Stop hiding. Dare to peek at the narrow road. Surrender completely—I'll catch you.

I stood on the tallest rock and scanned the ocean's churning black water, then took a closer look at the way down to the beach. To climb down safely, I'd have to jump across a small gap in the rocks. It might as well have been a yawning abyss. My legs shook uncontrollably.

I groped my way along the precipice, barking my shin on a rock that jutted out, tasting the danger of crashing waves. Death would be easy, I thought. One false step and I'd know for sure whether the story was true. I had to act, though, to get to the other side. I closed my eyes and leapt.

Something caught me. My foot slid on a patch of gravel, I grabbed for a branch and went to my knees, but I didn't fall. The cloak wrapped me again in my childhood, but this time, death wasn't frightening. While the gravel bit into my knees I stayed there, clutching the branch for dear life, hanging on to my childhood Jesus in an attitude of surrender.

"God, please tell me it's all true," I said to the roar of the ocean. "Show me what to do." In the dark I cried out loud. I sensed the real danger in crossing over to where Jesus stands, lamb about his shoulders, lion at his side. No matter whether I clothe God in brimstone, in Snoopy jokes, or in the confusing pantheon of those New Age gods, the decision has to be mine alone. Nobody can force me to have faith. Nobody can make me crucify my will or die to sin. Not even God.

I stayed out on that promontory longer than I should have. By the time I climbed down, it was pitch dark and very late. My husband would be worried. I'd already accepted the Son as my Savior, but I was a brand-new baby, stumbling along God's unexplored, wild path. Yet God climbed down with me that night. Jesus wrote me a faith that has wavered at times but has never disappeared.

My little white Bible is tattered and worn now, and I have a newer version with much bigger print. That old Bible still reminds me of Grandma Gypsy, in her brown hat with its netting, as she listened to a sermon about death. Life is so hazardous, even radioactive in its danger. My life requires prayer that can peel paint off a wall.

The Storm

LINDA: I can hear the storm raging, but I can't tell where it is.

KRIS: Inside you, maybe?

LINDA: Maybe, but there's one out there someplace. I've always thought that those nuts who chase tornadoes and hurricanes were crazy. But we probably look weird to people who aren't on the hunt for God. Yet.

KRIS: What I've always wondered is why some people never get that assignment. And they lead lives with almost no trouble in them.

LINDA: Meanwhile I'm hoping that God's storm doesn't wash me away.

KRIS: I think God looks like a storm. A tornado.

The Church and the World

KRIS

We had an elephant in our church. I don't know where he usually slept. He had most of his belongings stuffed into his sweater, so he had a shape like women of the 1890s, with an exaggerated chest and skinny legs. He carried a Bible and some other books, and he participated in our weekly communion service, obviously familiar with the procedure. He began parking his bike in our church lot and I think he often stayed out of the rain on our church's covered side porch.

Like most elephant-keepers, most people in our congregation didn't acknowledge his presence, but a few raved that at the coffee hour after church, he took too many cookies and too much cream and sugar in his coffee. They were furious about the amount of food he ate at church potlucks. To suggest that the meal might be his only certain food caused otherwise lovely Christian women to hold their noses, shake their fingers, and purse their angry lips.

His name was Verlyn, a dark-haired, thin man with what was almost a limp. Our family usually tried to guide him into a pew with us, because we knew some others were horribly offended by the presence of our elephant. Once he mentioned that it was his birthday, and my eight-year-old grandson said, "Well, happy birthday!" and gave Verlyn his entire allowance, a dollar in change.

I liked him. He sometimes sat beside me during the adult education hour and sometimes gave me some funny asides. Some of them related to the sermon and others were from voices in his head. One Sunday when we were discussing the problem of alcoholism in our society, he stood up to say, "I grew up in a car because my father was an alcoholic. We have to do something." Some Sundays he was less coherent, but he was always himself.

Most homeless people don't have access to showers and soap and laundries. Saying that soap is cheap is to ignore the fact that "cheap" isn't relevant when you have absolutely no money. Verlyn sometimes picked beans or berries for a bit of pay, but I never saw him buy more than a cup of coffee unless someone pressed money on him. Once I saw him shed tears after he made his communion; maybe for once, he was filled. My husband and I said we had Jesus coming to us in Verlyn's form, even if he was—as he always has been—a source of discomfort.

On Thanksgiving Day he came to the church service, and someone took him a six-pack of Spam, which had a pull-off lid and was fully cooked, so he didn't need a can opener or a stove. As I left church that day, I found him on the side porch, paring off pieces of the luncheon meat, gobbling them so fast he went through the first can in about a minute.

"Are you going to one of the dinners around town?" I asked. The rescue mission and several churches were holding free dinners. He shook his head.

"My bike has a flat tire and I can't walk that far," he said. I knew what I needed to do. God made it crystal clear what I should do; but instead, I pulled a twenty out of my wallet and told him to buy dinner at a local restaurant.

Our pastor was locking up the doors and he saw the scene on the porch. He smiled as I went back inside toward the backdoor and told me what a fine thing I had done.

"Are you kidding?" I stormed. "That was one of the worst things I've ever done. I was supposed to invite him home for dinner with our family."

Why hadn't I? First of all, my daughter-in-law had been assaulted by a stranger, and I'm sure the sight of Verlyn might bring it all back. She still reacted with terror in some circumstances. And second, Verlyn . . . well, Verlyn stank. Our happy family festivities, with not only wonderful food but one daughter's autumn centerpiece, another's homemade cheesecake, and my son's guitar playing, would all melt into a wonderful holiday that would end singing around the fireplace. But if Verlyn had been there, as an unknown element we weren't sure we trusted, a man who didn't know our family's speech shortcuts or know that we had to have two kinds of cranberry sauce because we had chosen up sides for each; if Verlyn had been there, with his terrible clothes and that sewer smell, he might have been the only one to have a good time.

At Christmas my daughter's family brought wrapped gifts for him, but they didn't mention that we were having a progressive family dinner the next day. My daughter bought him a new black sweater to replace the one he wore over his stuffing. I brought him a new lock for his bike and went home to fill stockings and drink some hot cider in front of our trees.

By the next spring, when Eugene had turned pink because the flowering crab apple and plum trees had gone into their yearly Easter celebrations, when the daffodils were almost over and weeping willow trees were bright, pale green, things came to a head in our church. Verlyn had piled some of his belongings in plastic bags around his bike in the parking lot, and members of the church board decided that those bags contained useless trash and that Verlyn had no value either. They threw all his stuff in the dumpster and informed the man that he was *persona no grata* at our downtown church.

I encountered the pastor that day in the church kitchen after a women's luncheon. He and I got about three inches from each other and began to yell, sometimes alternately and sometimes at the same time. I argued that trash or no, those bags were Verlyn's only belongings and that he was a guest God had sent us. Finally, the pastor mentioned that people were scared of Verlyn, and he said that some of our biggest pledgers and givers were uncomfortable with his presence.

I was even more appalled. "Oh sure," I said. "I think I read that story somewhere. You can sit at my feet, but you over there, with the big bankroll, take the seat of honor." I had to set down the stack of plates I'd been washing, for fear of dropping or even throwing them, plate by plate, against the wall or into my pastor's hard Irish head. "Probably he was Jesus," I yelled, and left.

I know others were disturbed about Verlyn's treatment, but I didn't call them. We certainly didn't need a church schism over the event. Or did we? Jesus is a gadfly sometimes. I heard Verlyn was going to the Presbyterian church, but when I drove around the area, I could never find him. After a while, we halfway forgot, and the pastor and I began speaking again; we were both wary and suspicious, though, circling each other like angry little dogs.

After a year, my denomination had a statewide early fall event in the outdoor stadium at the University of Oregon. Many people from our parish attended and were overwhelmed not only by the multichurch choir, the powerful prayers, and the inspiring sermons; they were also astonished to see Verlyn.

He wore a short-sleeved shirt and black jeans. His hair was cut and he glowed with cleanliness and health. The only thing he carried was the bulletin for the service, and he smiled and shook hands with everyone he remembered from our parish. Even our pastor.

Verlyn had spent the last few months in a city seventy miles south of us. He showed up for communion a few Sundays and partook of their after-church brunch. The pastor and board of that church discovered that Verlyn was homeless and had some physical and mental problems that kept him from working, so they took on the government and finally won monthly SSI payments for him, got him into an apartment, and helped him buy clothes. Parishioners invited him for dinners and cookouts and even camping trips; they found out that he was a fine fisherman and had a wealth of stories from his travels to entertain them.

Who was neighbor to that homeless man? I could have investigated Social Security disability, I could have taken him to a free or low-fee clinic and helped him find a place to live; instead, I had congratulated myself on being nicer to him than some others, handed him money, and left him in the cold.

What is our Christian responsibility? Should we hand out money to people with signs, offer breakfasts or soup kitchens, and take in the bedraggled leftovers of our society, people with shopping carts who come to our coffee hours to eat and get out of the rain or cold? Or maybe should we just, as some churches do, give them bus fare to the local rescue mission and then believe we've done our duty?

The matter is settled; Jesus says in Matthew 25:34–41:

Then the king will say to those at his right hand, "Come, you that are blessed by my Father, inherit the kingdom prepared for you from the foundation of the world; for I was hungry and you gave me food, I was thirsty and you gave me something to drink, I was a stranger and you welcomed me, I was naked and you gave me clothing, I was sick and you took care of me, I was in prison and you visited me." Then the righteous will answer him, "Lord, when was it that we saw you hungry and gave you food, or thirsty and gave you something to drink? And when was it that we saw you a stranger and welcomed you, or naked and gave you clothing? And when was it that we saw you sick or in prison and visited you?" And the king will answer them, "Truly I tell you, just as you did it to one of the least of these who are members of my family, you did it to me." Then he will say to those at his left hand, "You that are accursed, depart from me into the eternal fire prepared for the devil and his angels."

No matter how spiritual the message is, how anointed the preaching or how generous the contributions to the church building fund, if we have no charity or mercy toward the unwashed or unloved poor, our offerings are tinkling silver and sounding brass, noise made in public to attract the attention of passersby, who are the only audience. God might not be listening.

A Wounded Healer

KRIS: Did I say a storm in the church? Or an elephant. I guess it's my duty as an author to stand up for Jesus and declare God's prophecies about poverty.

LINDA: I think God did make you like a prophet in that way, which must be very hard.

KRIS: Not too bad, as long as you don't want to have any friends and don't mind being smacked around. Any minute now, they'll throw me in a cistern.

LINDA: But my calling feels different. When I stand up for Jesus, I know he wants me to serve a different way from prophesying.

KRIS: Your voice isn't loud enough for you to be a prophet. I think you're like a healer, Linda.

LINDA: How can I be like a healer? I still have a paralyzed arm.

KRIS: I think you're like a healer of fights and quarrels and people's relationships—a wounded healer, like Henri Nouwen.

LINDA: I heard about this girl at church . . .

The Arms of God

LINDA

That summer day, the church was warm. Folks fanned themselves with their bulletins. I almost wished I'd slept in. Then the sermon piqued my interest. The preacher began by asking, "What were you doing when you were nine years old?" She paused, then painted a picture of the average American childhood: jumping rope, pumping high on swings, and fishing with Granddad; raising a hand in school, running at recess, and laughing on sleepovers; eating ice cream, candy, and Happy Meals.

Do you remember your ninth summer? I shifted in the pew. How could I forget?

Before the preacher could continue, I saw myself at nine: in a Shriner's hospital, undergoing surgeries on my paralyzed left arm. Being nine wasn't much fun, as I recalled it, and I immediately set myself apart from the rest of the congregation. Who could possibly have had a ninth year like mine?

A moment later the preacher answered my question. Isra, that's who. She's a nine-year-old Iraqi girl, living out a situation so familiar to me it makes me squirm. The violence in her country has touched her—shrapnel from a mortar recently ripped off her right arm. One minute she's having the best Iraqi childhood she can in a dangerous time of war. The next her head and abdomen are riddled with shrapnel and just below her shoulder, her arm is gone. Gone.

Now, the preacher said, Isra needs help getting to the United States to be fitted with her expensive-but-donated prosthesis at a Shriner's hospital. I'm sure my mouth dropped open. I hadn't seen that one coming.

The preacher gave a list of reasons why we ought to help Isra. Her classmates tease her to the point that Isra no longer wants to attend school. Without the prosthesis she might never be able to make a living, and it's implied that she'll have cultural difficulties because of the stigma surrounding disability. Worst of all, Isra has terrible nightmares as she tries to make sense of all that has befallen her.

I'm almost certain that everyone in that church gave generously, for the plight of a nine-year-old, as well as for the healing of our two nations. God nudged me to donate to the Isra Project but also dared me to think about the one-armed girl in a way I rarely grant to my own disability. Think healing, God said. I cannot refuse.

Dear God, heal Isra, I pray over and over. Make her whole. And dear God, can you please make it the very best healing possible and also really soon?

Healing—what a touchy subject for many Christians! Red hot and dangerous. Although most of us are reading the same Scriptures, many branches of our faith disagree on this subject. One camp insists on certain rituals or methods, while those in an opposing camp shrug and say God's will is all that matters. Some believe in signs and wonders extending to miraculous physical healings, while others concentrate on getting the soul and the spirit right with God.

Inside, though, aren't most of us dying to crash into the throne room and demand to know exactly what we're supposed to do to receive inner or outer healings? I know I am.

If only Jesus were still walking around, healing people everywhere! He said we should have the faith of a grain of mustard to be healed, but nobody has ever figured out exactly how to cram faith into anything, much less a tiny seed. On some occasions I know God's healing touch has brushed against me. At other times I cry and beg and promise to do this or that, but no cure appears, suffering isn't abated. I feel as if all hell has broken loose. I wonder if Isra feels that way sometimes too.

Most of the time I don't know what to believe about modern-day physical miracle healings. I confess there's one part of me that desperately wants reports of regrown limbs or restored sight to be true. Then the realistic me harrumphs, "Not likely!" A third me lands somewhere in between, confident that with God nothing is impossible but worried I might not want to hold my breath when it comes to God healing me. My faith seems to be the central issue, faith that I find lacking, and some days, downright pathetic.

On one such day in the early 1980s, I was working in a Christian bookstore in Southern California. A pair of older women came into the store, where I stood restocking greeting cards on a display. The two browsed for a few minutes and then one of them sidled up to me and whispered, "If you only had a little more faith, God would heal that arm!" Then they left, as mysteriously as they had come. I couldn't move for a long time, frozen by the woman's chilling advice. A little more faith? What on earth is it and how do I get some?

Those words still echo in my memory, still clomp across the garden of my very fragile faith. Yet in a way the woman made sense, seeing as how I usually believe everything is my fault. I must do something to be healed, and of course, I have failed again.

The concept of grace teaches me that I can't do anything to lose or win God's favor. But if I concentrate on buffing up my faith to gain an arm that does what a good arm should, it follows that God would grant my wish. He might upgrade my eyesight and a few other things while he's at it.

Seventies evangelist Kathryn Kuhlman, whose miracle services claimed thousands of healings, said, "Wonderful as physical healing is, it's secondary to the healing of the soul." She often concluded her standing-room-only sessions with a call for salvation. I can't argue that eternal life should be high on everyone's list, but many a sick person would settle for ordinary life with no pain, days filled with joy not suffering, life with two arms not one, the right to be a normal, innocent nine-year-old.

Innocents who suffer at the hands of humans or disease or weather have always been problems for serious Christians. We can't understand the logic of our world. Greedy and violent persons live full, satisfied lives, while war, pestilence, and disease kill or maim babies and children. As Philip Yancey asked in the title of one of his books, Where is God when it hurts?

I've read everything I can find on the subject. Many authors point to the Old Testament and compare contemporary suffering to the Israelites, who couldn't obey God and thus endured punishment after punishment. Other writers refer to the book of Job. He wasn't guilty of much, but God chose to make an example of poor old Job. I think about putting my own trials into perspective. When you feel as if nobody's ever suffered the way you're suffering, just read about Job. Be grateful you have no boils. If you happen to be covered in boils, be thankful nothing worse has happened.

That's not what God meant, of course. When it comes to risky subjects like healing, I wonder if any human really knows what God means. St. Paul says that for now, "we see through a glass darkly," so maybe understanding the "right" way to go about healing doesn't exist.

Tell that to Isra and your friend with terminal cancer, your sister with the migraines, the son with mental illness. Tell your mom whose fingers, gnarled from arthritis, resemble twisted manzanita twigs. Or tell your father, frozen by Lou Gehrig's disease, your aunt staring blankly from Alzheimer's. Tell anyone who tries to cope with sickness that God is hidden, a mystery, that Jesus healed anyone who asked him but these days we aren't sure how to ask. Tell me that we just don't know or that I need more faith. The garden of hope wilts and dies. I'm sicker than ever.

So what can we do? We can employ prayer shawls and rags, touch sacred sand, anoint with oil, and lay on hands. We can douse ourselves with holy water, light candles and incense, go to church day and night, read the Bible, or seek out a modern Kathryn Kuhlman. I don't think it matters what you use as much as it matters that you care.

We can care for Isra and for one another, with our time and our money, our prayers and our love. All these things may comfort, and as long as they don't harm anyone, they may increase our faith. For me, the only sure thing is to pray and pray and pray some more. Sometimes I'm awed by healing—even if it's a headache. Other times I must lift my good arm in praise to God even though there is no evidence of change.

Please, dear God, when you get a minute, could you help Isra get to Florida? Thanks a lot.

I believe that any hour, any minute, any second now, Jesus will return. Millions will flock to his side, hoping to touch the hem of his garment. I'll be among them, ready to be shot through with Jesus's love. Until then, I will keep praying, for Isra, for all those with illness or troubles, for my faith to increase.

And I'll do what I can, whether it's to help a nine-year-old Iraqi girl or pray for anyone who is sick, in body, mind, or spirit. I may never receive a supernatural healing for my paralysis, but by extending a hand to others, I strengthen my mental and spiritual well-being. Even though God doesn't always do what I think he should, I can't stop believing in his power to heal. I may not truly feel your pain, but I can pray for your healing. And the more I pray for others, the better I feel. From the bookstore woman's words to the pain of surgeries at age nine, I pray for Isra, and my own burden lightens. That's a miracle in itself.

Isra taught me that the world is small, that we're all connected. She knows what I know, that a one-handed life is hard, and yet I can't stop there. I give to her cause; I pray; I imagine her fortified by compassion. I love her from afar, and I decide we should help each other because we can, because this is real love, God's love, enfolding us like giant comforting arms.

A Lightning Strike

LINDA: I still don't know whether Isra got to Florida. But God is directing my attention somewhere else now. God is always on the move, like a thunderstorm, and always wants to take you along. I just wish I knew for sure where we were going.

KRIS: Sometimes lightning just dances around, raking the atmosphere, tearing it up. I've been on hikes where we suddenly had to squat with our hands on our knees and duckwalk on the balls of our feet because the electrical charge was making our skin tingle or our hair stand on end. I haven't been struck yet but I've been scared.

LINDA: Neither have I, but sometimes life makes me feel as if I had been. Every time my kids have problems, I feel . . .

KRIS: Amazed. You feel amazed. The root of that word means "confused."

LINDA: You mean all those choirs have been singing "Confusing Grace"?

[Short period of laughter.]

KRIS: Grace *is* confusing. We don't understand how it works or why. Some of the gospel stories sound like conditional grace, for instance the parable of the talents, but others sound as if grace is perpetual. Some theologians say we're either eternally secure in Christ or salvation by grace is an error.

LINDA: I think you receive grace only as a lightning strike from God. Let's see if I've got this straight. Grace is confusing and dangerous, and we're either secure or we're not.

KRIS: The theologian Reinhold Niebuhr said we have to live in the tension between law and grace. And I think God's lightning strikes between them.

LINDA: Because we wouldn't know grace if we hadn't had a brush with the Old Testament law.

KRIS: Niebuhr also said that when people forgive one another, the tension between law and grace is resolved in their lives. The sin was against law, but forgiveness is grace.[24]

LINDA: So lightning must be the decision you make. I get it! You can go all the way to law and be a mean little judge. Or go all the way to grace and pretend you don't hurt. Or you can follow God's lightning and recognize the law while offering grace.

KRIS: God is more than maybe.

LINDA: If grace is a lightning strike from God, then what is above it? What's on the other side?

KRIS: Either God is up there like Zeus, hurling lightning, or there's only a thin membrane between us and God, between us and eternity.

LINDA: Is that why, in the Old Testament, the Holy of Holies had a veil in front of it?

KRIS: But Christ ripped the veil. So now we see the same thing Titus saw when the Romans invaded the temple. Nothing.

LINDA: Nothing and everything.

KRIS: I think what we see is a decision.

LINDA: You mean the decision that God made when he created us?

KRIS: I mean the decision to see. You can either look around and see God or stay blind.

MAKING PEACE WITH A DANGEROUS GOD

An Invitation

LINDA: You once spoke of falling into God, like falling into the surface of the sun.

KRIS: And since the surface of the sun has no crust, when you let yourself fall, you go straight to the core. A hot trip but better than anything you've ever known: heated white, burning, eternally burning with the love of God.

LINDA: And dangerous.

KRIS: Anything that can consume you, burn you up, is dangerous. At least to the ego. You can't try to conserve your ideas or your personality when you're surrendering. Can you?

LINDA: Whenever I try to hold anything back from God, he hunts me down.

KRIS: Like what?

LINDA: I try to lie to myself, and God, about how I feel about my kids, my career, even my marriage. I've discovered, however, that trying to lie to God is a no-win situation.

KRIS: Well, but it's a no-lose situation too. When God says, "Come, get burned alive," God is inviting you to immortality. But we can't cross into God's country yet.

God's T-Shirt

KRIS

Today the CNN webpage shows a distraught, weeping woman who clutches to her bosom a T-shirt that belonged to her dead son. He was killed in a fire, and she was kneeling at his grave. Are his shirts and tombstone all she has of him now? Of course not. She has the memory of his tiny infant mouth at her breast, memories of the thousand times she washed his hands and face. She knows the sound of his voice and will always remember it, and though she grieves her loss, she will never really lose her vision of her son. But for today, maybe even for a few weeks, the shirt is an intimate reminder, perhaps warm from the dryer, or an unwashed one with his scent in the cloth. For now, she needs the physical. We all do sometimes. We really want to taste and see that the Lord is good. We want to see a photograph of God, hear a recording of God's voice, clutch God's T-shirt to our bosom, while we long for his presence.

When we were in Israel, a guide showed us what he said were the very water jars at Cana. Were any of these containers authentic? Well, they were actual first-century artifacts, which lent them an air of credibility, but I doubt they had anything to do with a miracle. I doubt on two counts. First, the host at the wedding probably used his water jars daily, had no idea that anything Jesus touched would have value, and would have treated them like ordinary household containers.

But second, and this is more important, we can't see the real jars because God doesn't want us attaching our faith to things. Or places. Nobody knows where Moses is buried, the location of Jesus's temporary tomb is uncertain, the furor over the Shroud of Turin keeps scholars guessing, and nobody has dug up Joseph's carpentry tools. We are instructed not to make graven images, which means that we can't venerate objects or places.

A treasury of relics amassed during the time of the Byzantine Empire included some milk from the breast of the Virgin Mary, the teeth of St. Christopher, and alleged bodily remains of biblical figures, as well as Old Testament relics, such as the trumpet blown by Joshua at Jericho and even the tablets of the law given to Moses by God. All these objects appeared miraculously in churches and caves and odd sacred spots.

I'm troubled by the physical. Yes, I have a Mexican crucifix, a gift from my daughter, on my office wall, and Palm Sunday fronds stuck here and there. I even have an icon calendar. But none of those things is holy, or at least not holy because someone touched it or blessed it or wore it. God did say, "You shall not make for yourself an idol, whether in the form of anything that is in heaven above, or that is on the earth beneath, or that is in the water under the earth. You shall not bow down to them or worship them" (Deut. 5:8–9).

I think God gets nervous about our expeditions to find Noah's ark on the mountains of Ararat and the attempts to discover whether the Ethiopian church really owns the Ark of the Covenant they say is behind the curtains. There's a reason why Michael the Archangel contended with the devil about the body of Moses, a reason why we can't find the Holy Grail, a reason why we'll never find the site of Eden. It's because physical objects that represent God can fool you, can make you think you need them to worship. And you can't confine the Spirit to a tabernacle or a communion cup or a fresco. People—even some scientists—had their hearts broken by the revelation that the Shroud of Turin was a piece of medieval cloth, and some of them are still trying to discredit or disprove that carbon 14 evidence. I had said for years that I wished it would self-destruct so people wouldn't get hurt.

God's ordinance forbids the making of images. The Jewish Holy Scriptures reveal the second commandment as follows: "You shall not make a carved image nor any likeness of that which is in the heavens above or on the earth below or in the water beneath the earth. You shall not prostrate yourself before them nor worship them, for I am Hashem your God—a jealous God" (Exod. 20:4–6).

God made the rule clear: Don't make it; don't venerate it. But from the beginning of our faith, we've begged to break that rule. Even while Moses was on the mountain receiving the commandments, his flock, aided by Aaron, was melting their earrings down to make a golden calf. I've always loved Aaron's nonconfession. He told Moses the people begged for a god, so he said, "I said to them, 'Whoever has gold, take it off'; so they gave it to me, and I threw it into the fire, and out came this calf!'" (Exod. 32:24). We want images—statues, paintings, sacred pools, magnificent cathedrals—which are all fine if they aid your worship but don't become its object.

Sometimes we just open our Bibles, not only because they contain the truth, but because they're physical objects as well as spiritual ones; we want something we can see and touch. And even the Bible isn't always physical enough for us. We're always looking for the secret document that will be the twenty-ninth chapter of Acts or something in Jesus's handwriting or maybe even the original accounting of Paul's conversion.

And if every Bible on earth were burned in bonfires worthy of *Fahrenheit 451*, we would do as the people of that novel and movie did: We would memorize and recite the Word. A few years ago I taught at a conference where a Methodist scholar named H. Bogart Dunne lectured on the Gospel of Mark without any text or notes. We finally asked him to recite the entire Gospel, and he did, from memory. Now there's a relic—carrying the Word around inside yourself, like a love letter pressed against your vagus nerve.

Halfway through his recitation, which was in no way theatrical or a performance, I could feel tears running down my cheeks. Bogart was enough of a purist about the original text that he stopped at "and they said nothing to anyone, for they were afraid" (Mark 16:8). As soon as he was finished, I raced to my cabin, to shed more tears and to hold the sound of the words within me as if I were a bell whose clapper bonged through my brain and rib cage and hollow spots in my bones.

Holding on is a pleasant impulse but dangerous. On the Mount of Transfiguration, the moment was so delicious, so perfect, with Jesus talking to Moses and Elijah, that Peter wanted to erect a memorial of that day by putting up three tabernacles. He began talking so nothing would change. It took a voice from heaven to quiet Peter. And Mary Magdalene, her eyes swollen from so much weeping, wanted to cling to Jesus after his resurrection, to make the moment last forever, but Jesus whispered, "Don't hang on me, Mary. I have to ascend to my Father."

Nowadays we don't worship calves, but we do love our symbols. I'm a big symbol person, and when I was stringing some turquoise and coral for a necklace, I added in a few blue-and-white God's Eye beads I bought in Istanbul. That way I could remind myself who was watching me and who was in charge. And if they warded off the evil eye, well, that would be great.

But we don't need symbols or pictures to think about God, about Jesus. We couldn't forget about God even if every cross or altar or trumpet on earth were destroyed. If the cross were forbidden in our society, we would still have the cross of Christ emblazoned in our souls. Some scholars think the sign of the cross—made by touching your fingers to your forehead, heart, and shoulders—may have originated during times when the Romans persecuted the church, when crosses were hidden, forbidden by the emperor of Rome.

People who travel a lot like to buy souvenirs and take pictures; people on spiritual journeys pick things up too, as if to preserve their trips with photographs and figurines and bracelet charms. I always want to bring my experience into the house, to hold on to the moment. I have some acorns that dropped from oak trees in Turkey, a chip of pottery from Rome, a black, round stone I picked up at a retreat twenty years ago, a hunk of Resurrection plant (a dry Spanish moss that turns bright green and soft when you wet it). My favorite souvenirs are books—guides to cities and museums but also guides to the spirit life.

We're having serious wildfires here in Oregon, some from lightning and others started by arsonists. Homeowners in danger are carrying photo albums and cats and dogs out to their cars, driving away at the last minute. I'm sure some of them grabbed their dog-eared Bibles, because people take what's most precious to them when fire threatens.

But what if a fire burned up everything on earth? What if all we had were those Bible reciters and a lot of veldt and desert and savannah and tundra? What if I could never read again or look at the brass cross in my church or see the brilliant fresco of the Anastasis in Istanbul?

Well, I think I'd sit down, close my eyes, and look backward at my journey while I clutched something like a T-shirt to my breastbone. Just until its Owner comes for it.

Peace with God

KRIS: We're winding down, kiddo. I'm almost out of clever things to say. But while I'm clutching that T-shirt, I'm also pleading for peace in the world.

LINDA: Is there a difference between world peace and peace with God? Peace with a *dangerous* God?

KRIS: I know people who are ostensibly at peace with God but who believe in just wars—or any wars, when America is fighting.

LINDA: If we live as Jesus told us to live, we must love God and our neighbors.

KRIS: That was Christ's instruction to the Jews, and it's the instruction we hear most in church. But he said to his followers, "I give you a new commandment, that you love one another. Just as I have loved you, you also should love one another." *And he was willing to die for you.*

LINDA: What if you could dive through that spiritual membrane into peace?

KRIS: Does peace with God mean peace in the world?

LINDA: Well, it has to start with you. Or with me.

Not as the World Gives

LINDA

Peace I leave with you; my peace I give to you. I do not give to you as the world gives. Do not let your hearts be troubled, and do not let them be afraid.

John 14:27

On a balmy late-summer evening I power walk through my neighborhood. Above me, the fiery reds and dusky pinks of a Northwest sunset put on a show. The sweetness of blackberry bushes perfumes the air—I can almost taste the wind. A fragile orange tinge has already appeared on some of the oak leaves, and twice I have heard geese honking across the sky. Change is in the air. If I stay up late this week, I can watch the Pleiades meteor showers splash the heavens. Everywhere I look God is there, inviting me, no urging me, to cross over through the Peace Gate.

But this gate is like the Mercy Gate in Jerusalem that the Suleiman Muslims boarded so the Messiah couldn't enter. The Peace portal is dark and, although the name sounds tame, wild things are rumored to lurk in the shadows. God promises me that Jesus waits for me on the other side of the threshold.

But to get there, to Peace, I've got to decide to take that first step. The distance is both microscopic and immense and only requires a flight of the mind. Do I trust God to be there when I step through?

Too many things about life are still a mystery to me. Allying myself with a God who runs the universe in ways I can't understand still seems risky, some days futile. The oppressed of the world hang all their hopes on a soon and very soon gospel and an unlikely story of God becoming a man and then sacrificing himself for the world. How do the downtrodden do it? What do they know?

I wish I could say for sure.

My stride slows down—I can't help thinking about some of the problems I've written about. Pain reminds me that my chronic post-polio syndrome is acting up, that some of my family members battle addiction, that I wage my own war with codependence. Kristen's grandson has cancer.

All over America, couples are divorcing, going bankrupt, or shooting each other. Africans are starving or being massacred; the Middle East is an awful mess. I stop on the side of the street to catch my breath. The calamities of the world make it hard to see where the opening to the Peace Gate lies.

But God won't let me quit. I get going again, hopping over a puddle left by a wayward lawn sprinkler. My arms pump in the rhythm of prayer: end wars, feed the starving, keep me going. Please make Andy well, grant my son healing from his addiction, give me strength to get around the block. My pace quickens and I gasp for breath. Power walking, like following Christ, can be hard work.

For some of you, the race is second nature. You're like Kristen—as far back as you remember you've always believed. Sometimes you've doubted, but you always held on to a sliver of faith. Maybe you've shaken your fist in God's direction, especially if your loved one suffers some horrible disease or goes missing or dies. But no matter what, some of you are like Kristen, confident that God is real, that Jesus did all he said, and that eternal life awaits you.

Others of you may be more like me: growing up searching for God, Protestant but basically unchurched, wandering off into New Age or worse only to come full circle, deciding that Christianity ultimately requires a leap of faith, making that leap, no matter how dangerous, yet a little unsure of what lies ahead, unsure you qualify for God's love.

As usual, I round a particular street corner, and behind a wood fence, the same three dogs bark furiously at me. I laugh; one of the dogs stares at me through a knothole, his one glassy eye making sure I don't escape his gaze. I feel like barking back, but instead I call out, "Hi boys." I come by here often, after all. That one dog never fails to peek through the hole.

Making peace with a dangerous God feels a lot like my power walks. Some days my energy flags. Some days being a Christian feels to me as predictable as the dog behind the knothole. Often I wonder if I'll ever get any sort of lasting peace. You get through one of life's hurdles only to face the next challenge. I want to scream, "Enough, already!" only to panic at the thought of God giving up on me.

The seventh beatitude says, "Blessed are the peacemakers, for they will be called children of God" (Matt. 5:9). Charles Spurgeon wrote that "peacemakers" comes after "blessed are the pure," because we are to be pure first and peaceable second, after the example of Jesus.

"However peaceable we may be in this world, yet we shall be misrepresented and misunderstood: and no marvel, for even the Prince of Peace, by his very peacefulness, brought fire on the earth."[25]

Becoming "pure" is part of the danger we face as Christians—are we to come to God as "filthy rags" with heads hanging in shame? Or are we to declare that Jesus is the propitiation for our sins and cry out, "Abba! Father!"? I wrote about my confusion with Jesus's statement to be perfect, "as I am perfect." That verse hung over me as an indictment until I learned that "perfect" means compassion, not minding p's and q's. As I step along, I ask God for more compassion and promise to help those in need. God's peace looms ahead, and it's getting closer with every stride.

A common saying declares, "Christianity is not a destination—it's a journey." The Christian walk implies movement not stagnation. As in John Bunyan's *The Pilgrim's Progress*, Kristen and I are making the trip, and like Christian, we've learned the road is fraught with peril and hidden pitfalls—despondency, worldly cares, even death. We've asked some difficult questions, hoping to learn more about our faith and ourselves. And you've come along, needing to make your own peace with the dangerous God.

We wanted to give you solid answers, but we found a wild thing called God prowling our lives with the sweet hot breath of a lover. The peace we were desperate to make turned out to be a priceless gift from God the lover. We must step forward to receive that gift.

All I can offer you, the reader, is my own precarious balance between dogma and experience. Like Symeon, an eleventh-century monk, I'm discovering that some of the structure I've chafed against is indeed a signpost of my emotional inner experiences with God. Without the inner experience, dogma is little more than empty words. But without an awareness of Christian principles, I could easily lose my way in the land of "subjective experience." As one Christian writer said, the church is not an institution arbitrarily forcing us to follow its rules, but a community inviting us to still our hunger and thirst for the Truth at its table.

I set out to find solutions to the hidden mystery of God, and this journey has led me to compare faith notes with some remarkable believers. I've gone outside my own comfort zone to expand my understanding—including a new interest in the Bible, a more active prayer life, and even exploring new ways of worship.

Writer Frederica Mathewes-Greene echoes my own longing when she says, "The holy, invisible Lord surrounds us and we grasp for his elusive presence, kneeling down awestruck with our foreheads to the floor, tasting heaven on the Eucharistic spoon, laying kisses on His image and each other and most anything else we can get hold of."[26] In liturgy and ceremony I've found comfort and assurance that the biggest danger I face from God is that love will burn me alive.

God is in some ways as mysterious to me now as when I began. I will admit that for me, questions still outnumber answers. I don't understand why God doesn't prevent disasters if he cares so much for us, or how come he isn't more like Santa Claus. Loving a hidden God is frustrating, even if the little man behind the curtain has no power. The world is as beautiful and terrifying as Frederick Buechner predicted, and it's sometimes hard not to quake with fear.

Yet two thousand years ago, something happened, some One happened that couldn't be explained away. Somehow the God of Israel waits for his beloved on the other side of the gate. Early church martyrs, the slave underground of the Civil War era, Holocaust victims, and present-day oppressed peoples have all clung to Jesus, abandoning reason and safety. All made a leap of faith of their own volition, having seen and heard the Good News. I'm on my own trek to where Jesus is, even if the dogs bark at me as I go by.

Finally, at twilight, I reach home. The birds have all quieted down, as I pull off my shoes and savor a long drink of water. I'm tired, but it's a good tired—I feel energized, no longer as afraid.

Kristen and I said at the beginning of this book that we both believe and love God. We've gotten to know him by different routes, but both of us have ended up at much the same spot, one of redis-covery. Somewhere along the way, as I have rediscovered God, I've changed. God's still dangerous, but I'm more irresistibly drawn to him than ever.

Relationship with this most dangerous God is not about one single act but a daily renewal. Get moving—rediscovering God takes energy and action, even if the action is surrender and stillness. Peace is not the absence of violence, a nonaction pact we forge with the Almighty. Peacemaking is more like a gift—a gift of a path that God lovingly sets before us.

The Adventure

LINDA: Peace doesn't always mean the absence of conflict. Jesus said he brought not peace but a sword.

KRIS: A sword to cut between what the world gives and God's gifts of love and wisdom?

LINDA: The picture of Jesus, meek, mild, and suffering, isn't the whole story. There's more.

KRIS: We prefer the meek Jesus because he doesn't scare us. The terrifying picture is the one by Michelangelo in which his hand is raised in the Last Judgment. He's huge, undisguised, beardless, and when his hand falls, the world, the universe will end.

LINDA: But in the meantime, Jesus invites us to adventure, doesn't he?

KRIS: Yes. There are always portraits of Christ, undiscovered aspects of his personality. We keep finding new pictures. But people shouldn't get so hooked on peace that they miss the excitement.

White Water

KRIS

We live near the McKenzie River, which begins as a little outlet of Clear Lake, in the Cascade foothills. By the time it tumbles into Springfield, Oregon, where I live, it shouts over the stones in its path and finally empties into the mighty Willamette, which flows north to the Columbia. The McKenzie rapids are so amazing, the little falls and deep swirls so white and frothy that people in wetsuits take their kayaks and rubber rafts into the river every summer day. They wear wetsuits because even in summer the water is so cold that if you fell in, you'd probably die of hypothermia before you drowned or anyone could rescue you.

I know a lot of people who won't try spiritual rapids. They stay on big lakes or wide, quiet rivers, occasionally stirring the oars or dragging their fingers in the water. They want to see trout jump between the water lilies, and they play guitars in the boats and feel soft breezes. Theirs is a gentle spirituality, a sure thing. Of course, there are people on the other extreme, the puritanical types who spend their lives trying to round the Horn in a sailboat during a hurricane. They may be brave, but they don't have much fun.

White-water rafting is fun, if scary. It's worse than a roller coaster, because even an experienced raft river guide can get a few yards off

225

course and head into the boulders. A subordinate rower like me could cause the raft to veer or even capsize. Somebody gets killed on the McKenzie every summer, but we go back, unable to resist the rush of the icy water as it plunges over ancient volcanic rock. Douglas firs and white alders line the banks, and occasionally a stony spit emerges, where courageous fishermen stand on the rocks to fly cast for trout, steelhead, and salmon. The dark green forest, snow-capped peaks, and the song of the river are irresistible. You will most likely see deer and elk, bucks in the velvet, sometimes running in packs of ten or more to race you on their path by the river. Bald eagles and ospreys dip for fish, sometimes almost close enough to touch, and beavers or muskrats stop working for a moment to see whether you're a friend or enemy or food thief. Blue jays and ravens order you out of their territory, sometimes arguing about which of them is the true king of the world.

And running the spiritual rapids is fun, if you can swallow your fear and trust your guide, who may command you to row or sit absolutely still or lean for ballast. When you first climb aboard, you'll feel the river moving beneath you and hear the roar; and you realize that being stationary isn't the natural state of things on the river.

A noted river guide wrote the following for future rafters:

Nearing the first rapid your pulse quickens. You hear your guide call that fateful command, "All hard forward!" The raft lunges into the maelstrom. The river tosses it left, right, and up. It plunges down. The force of your paddle against the water holds you inside the raft, against twisting, pulling, and pushing forces of inertia. The waves splash over your head. Gasping for air between blasts of water you can hear your guide steadfastly calling his commands; finding the weaknesses of the river and using the river's own strengths against itself. Suddenly everything is calm. You have made it through the first rapid.[27]

The trip isn't over yet, but your spiritual life is changed forever. You can't return to the placid lake, because the memory of the white water will always draw you. Once the initial excitement passes, you realize that riding the rapids with God means living the unexpected—and trusting. Because if you get in God's craft, if you trust the divine River Guide to get you through the white water and maybe over the falls, who will rescue you if you fall out? On the McKenzie, even good swimmers who jumped in to save their children or friends have died because of the rough rapids and water temperature—the same way Jesus came to rescue us from the grip of sin and the law and threw himself onto the cross.

Oddly enough, my first foray into the spiritual rapids was taking a class in New Testament Greek. Of course, we have no "originals" of the Gospels and Epistles, but getting a little closer to the language in which they were written meant that the texts came alive. Instead of knowing all about Jesus, I began to know him, to understand how irresistible he is, and to follow him wherever he led me. I learned Christian meditation and *lectio divina*, which is the contemplative Bible reading practiced in monasteries and by millions of believers all over the world. I began to investigate Jewish biblical literature and the Talmud. Every new study or interest made life with God more amazing until I finally began to pray almost all the time.

Give Christ an inch and he'll take at least a yard and more like a thousand miles. All you have to do is stand on the banks and next thing you know, you're bouncing around in a rubber raft, hoping you won't crash into the boulders. So the more I studied, the more I wanted to know. The more I prayed, the more desperately I sought prayer. I traveled to Jerusalem and Athens, Corinth, Damascus, Cairo, and Rome, all significant to Christians; and I did so with a spirit of adventure, hoping to find more than what our guides showed us, longing most of all to see God face-to-face instead of just learning words about him.

And because God doesn't give you a stone when you ask for bread, I began to see God's handiwork, not only in creation but in other people and dogs and paintings and history. Stories that weren't about God became stories about God. I began to wake in the middle of the night and discover I had been praying aloud in my sleep. God taught me through the Hubble space photographs and ancient poetry and shapes of mountains. Lines of Scripture began to dance in my brain, offering me new pictures about their meaning. The momentum of God became the rhythm of my life.

And the risk? Is it really dangerous to study more, to try to learn Hebrew, to meditate on the *Yod-Hey-Vav-Hey* of God's name? Is it scary to say a breath prayer night and day or to sit for hours in a Russian Orthodox church, reaching to learn about the transfiguration of Christ by gazing at an icon? Behold, I tell you a mystery: It's no longer how much you learn; God still flirts and teases, saying come a little closer, Kris, go into that church or read that book, talk to that scholar or monk or holy woman, dance for God in an Israeli or Yemeni step, collect pictures of crosses and hang them over your desk. Throw everything out of your life that isn't about me, God says, and make what you must keep, such as cooking or cleaning, new ways of doing your prayers. And when you answer God's invitation, something happens. Yes, it's scary, dangerous, and a threat to your everyday life because you can't hold on to it.

Jewish tradition says that every letter in every word of the Torah has a dancing angel connected to it. Oh, to see those angels dancing for God! Oh, to make those holy words come alive! Oh, to ride the rapids with Christ, through this life and then beyond it! Holiness means teetering on the edge of reality, finally leaving the world behind and sailing into the core mystery of who God is.

An Only Child

LINDA: It's so wonderful to think that God is a mystery, but one that is totally in love with me. Somehow, I'm different. It's as that old hymn says, "O Joy that seekest me through pain, I cannot close my heart to Thee."[28]

KRIS: I think writing this book has made us both different. The rabbis say that every word of Hebrew has an angel dancing on it. Maybe English has angels too.

LINDA: When we started, my ideas about God were rooted in childhood, filled with the hurts and fears that I, like many people, carried into adult life. It was so hard to get over the idea that God didn't like me.

KRIS: The most amazing part is that each of us is an "only child" to God. God loves you as if only you existed.

LINDA: I've handed my life over to God, but I had to revise my portrait of him.

A Portrait of Christ: Lions and Tigers and . . . Who?

LINDA

When I think about what Jesus looks like, the all-too-familiar paintings and Sunday school pictures scroll across my mind. Here he is, knocking at the door. There he is, hanging on the cross. Then there's that one in which Jesus's eyes seem to follow you as you walk across the room. He beckons little children to sit on his lap and is often shown as the Good Shepherd, with fuzzy lambs at his feet.

Are any of these true portraits of Christ?

When I was in the Crippled Children's Hospital for months at a time, any image of Jesus where light beams emanated from his halo was especially comforting to me. I'd imagine the light shooting straight into my heart, so I could sing "Jesus wants me for a sunbeam" with confidence. My early interest in rocket ships and outer space also gave me hope that those sunbeams might be special healing rays too. In the hospital I slept with my Bible under my pillow, so gentle Jesus, meek and mild, would know where I was.

I must have dozed off a lot, though, because if Jesus stopped by my hospital bed or sent healing rays, I don't remember. To me, the Lamb of God was more like a wild animal. In fact, instead of a nice soft Son of God, Jesus has been an untamed beast, prowling my life.

Sometimes Jesus is a bear. If I leave garbage lying around the campsite of my life, Ursa Major wants to wipe it out. Bear Jesus bursts on the scene and upends my picnic basket. His bear claws tear into all my precious secrets. He seems to enjoy Ding Dongs, Ho-Hos, Twinkies—and sins I can't resist, like envy, unforgiveness, or being judgmental.

The friend who's a bear in my life may not know who she is. On occasion I get my feelings hurt from the suggestions she hands out, as well as her bearish penchant for quoting Scripture. But like Bear Jesus, she instructs with comfort—meaning strength not consolation—and she has a way of looking straight through me to get at the real problem. She has a "mother grizzly" attitude about prayer for those in need. Knowing this grizzly of a Christian strengthens me.

The Jesus bear is smart and adaptable, and I have a terrible time fooling him too. He roars sometimes, but he's also charming and huggable. And he has a way of turning the worst things in my life into good.

John Stackhouse, of Regent College in Vancouver, British Columbia, once said, "That same brilliantly adaptable God is at work throughout this sin-sick world, bringing beauty out of baseness, heroism out of holocaust, love out of loss—even salvation out of sacrifice. He calls us to believe and then do the same."[29]

Sometimes when he calls me, he's interested in dancing. Right after the Bear rummages through my private life and upsets my money-changing table of sin, he wants to dance? Dancing Bear swings me around, reminding me to watch one of his spectacular sunsets or boogie with the vacuum cleaner now and then. This

Jesus makes me laugh, lets me be goofy, and always surprises me with joy.

While Bear Jesus is bold and doesn't care how much of a racket he makes, Christ the Tiger[30] is stealthy and stalks me in the forests of the night. William Blake's poem, *The Tyger*,[31] gives me goose bumps when I imagine the picture of Jesus's fearful symmetry or the burning fire of his eyes. From Blake's immortal words I conjure a Jesus whose search for me is tireless, who pursues me with the patience of a magnificent Bengal, in order that I might feast on his love.

I've known a tiger or two, friends and loved ones who never give up on me, who act as if they have all the time in the world to love me and be loved. My husband is one, as are my children, and my dear friend, Patti, who died last year from cancer, who loved me in spite of everything.

One of the great cats in my life actually looks tigerish—an orange and white tabby named Oliver, with green marble eyes and one of the loudest purrs I've ever heard. If I have an awful day, Oliver rolls onto his back and kneads the air with his clumsy big paws. I take my cue and rub his belly, and he acts like I'm the best thing since tuna fish. The rumbles from Oliver's throat are a mystery—no one knows why cats purr—but he always makes me feel loved.

As far as I know, Jesus doesn't purr or ask for belly rubs, but I can always feel his eyes on me, especially when I'm running from him. I don't know why I turn my back on God, but sometimes I do. I get tired of waiting for answers to prayer, or I feel the need to justify something I know isn't right for me. That's when God hunts me down, insistent on granting me grace.

In the tall grass the Tiger says nothing and says everything. He waits; his fiery eyes blend perfectly with the stars of the heavens. God's infinite wisdom thunders across the sky, calling my name. I think, if I stay quiet, eventually God will find someone else to bother. But my legs cramp from crouching, my heart pounds so loud that even the field mice must hear. I stand, scan the night for a trace of those bright reflective eyes. Just when I think he's gone, Jesus the Tiger pounces, and I'm in love all over again.

Instead of asking me to join in a goofy dance, the Tiger whispers, "I am your hiding place, your tabernacle, God's ambassador. I am Emmanuel, God with us."

A lovely devotional book, *At the Name of Jesus*, outlines a whole year's worth of names for Christ, from A to Z. Complete with delicate hand-drawn borders, the short meditations run through the Alpha and Omega of Jesus. Jesus the Tiger recites his own names into every listening ear.

Like Rudyard Kipling's Shere Khan, this tiger Christ speaks to all the shadows in our world: the calamities, natural and man-made, the enmity, the disease and brokenness, famine, despair. Except that this Khan is more powerful than any storybook character, and his weapon is far more powerful than fang or claw. Our tiger Christ holds a burning sword and assails the enemy for our sake, interceding for us before God's throne. When the ocean lies before me and I am drowning, he says, "Don't worry; I can swim." I cling to the Tiger's back with all God's promises about Jesus on my lips, and he delivers me safely to shore.

On dry land, though, the dense jungle confronts me once again. Ahead, liana vines twist around the trees; monkeys howl through damp air; snakes probably hang in the branches, ready to strike. I shiver—it's all frightening. Then, a roar. And the Lion emerges.

Christ as a lion is elegant and regal. The lion Aslan, C. S. Lewis said, is Jesus as Man in the world, dying to redeem God's people and coming back to life before ascending into heaven. And I have a lion in my own life that reminds me so much of Aslan. My friend and fellow writer Heather Harpham Kopp said it first about our friend, the "older" woman. In *I Went to the Animal Fair*, Kopp writes, ". . . she was like a lion in my van. Not voracious. But like Aslan."

As Heather says so well, our friend is "not motherish. But she is mentorish. Wise. And slightly terrifying to me because she knows exactly who she is."[32]

She's my lion too, and I agree. She's wise and terrifying—much like the real Aslan. She looks through my evasions and excuses and sometimes I get furious with her. Once she even roared at me because I refused to stop mentioning a hurtful experience I'd had in church. I haven't yet had the courage to roar back at my lion friend, but she tells me often to believe in myself, to stand up for myself, examine my real self. Most of all, this lion urges me to grab the gifts God has given me and run with them—straight into Aslan's dangerous and loving jaws.

C. S. Lewis's lion portrait of Jesus symbolizes power and glory, the King of kings. Jesus Christ, the Son of Man, wields the branch of righteousness and if any of those snakes tries to get me, he promises he'll whack it good.

"Don't be afraid," Lion says, "I'm here; I'm with you." Although he is the king of beasts, Jesus the Lion is tender, merciful too—like a lamb only different. All about his head a million sunbeams radiate until God's special healing rays penetrate my soul. He's a bear, a tiger, a lion, and a lamb. Tendrils of Jesus's true vine reach out to redeem me, helping me recognize all the faces of Christ in everyone I meet.

God and the Great Bungee Jump

KRIS: Ready, set—wait. Do I really want to jump off safety and into God's mysterious invitation?

LINDA: I'm terrified, but I can't say no.

KRIS: The last lines of Annie Dillard's novel *The Living* has people gathered in the dark of night around a pond. One of the guys swings out on the rope and then drops *into the stars*. I want to jump into that pond.

LINDA: I love the idea of being on the rope swing with God, or jumping on a bungee cord he has the end of.

KRIS: Are you ever afraid God will let go?

LINDA: If there's one thing I've learned, it's that if I don't take risks with God, or trust God, I can't jump into eternity. I'd be too self-centered, looking inward for safety.

KRIS: I think you have to trust God to jump into reality too. I want to be a servant to others, but only God can show me how to do that. I want reality and eternity to be about the same things. Or maybe I should say the same Person.

LINDA: Martin Buber said somewhere in *I and Thou* that we see God only in dialogue with other people.

KRIS: Well, well, well. Is that what we've been doing? Trying to see God through a book-long dialogue?

LINDA: Absolutely! We know God is dangerous and can shock us or kill us, but we've got to tie God the Live Wire around our ankles.

KRIS: And we invite our readers to take this dive with us.

LINDA: It might be scary at times, but it is certain to be exhilarating.

KRIS: Okay. Ready.

LINDA: Set.

KRIS AND
LINDA: Jump!

Notes

1. Rowan Williams, *Written in the Dust* (Grand Rapids: Eerdmans, 2002), 6.

2. Heather Harpham Kopp, *I Went to the Animal Fair* (Colorado Springs: NavPress 1993), 127.

3. *Sola scriptura* (Latin for "Scripture alone") is one of five important slogans of the Protestant Reformation.

4. Frederick Buechner, *The Magnificent Defeat* (New York: Seabury Press, 1966), 26.

5. Ibid., 18.

6. Alice Miller, *The Drama of the Gifted Child* (New York: Basic Books, 1996), 27.

7. Dietrich Bonhoeffer, *The Cost of Discipleship* (New York: MacMillan, 1963), 45.

8. Thomas P. McDonnell, ed., *A Thomas Merton Reader* (New York: Image Books, 1974), 191.

9. Karen Karper, *Where God Begins to Be* (Grand Rapids: Eerdmans, 1994), 25.

10. Ibid., 77.

11. Efim Sversky, *Connection* (Institute of Psycho-Spiritual Therapy, 2004).

12. Kenneth Prior, from a quote on the Internet site "Truth and Things: An Apologetics Handbook," www.angelfire.com/paz/truthandthings/handbook.html, accessed on October 28, 2005.

13. A. H. Hartzog, in G. C. Berkouwer, *A Half Century of Theology* (Grand Rapids: Eerdmans, 1977), 29.

14. Martin Bell, *The Way of the Wolf* (New York: Seabury Press, 1970), 1.

15. Barry Lopez, *Of Wolves and Men* (New York: Scribner, 1979).

16. William James, *Writings 1902–1910* (New York: Library of America, 1988), 22.

17. Emmanuel Levinas, response to Yossel Rakover's *Appeal to God*, from website "Jewish Theological Seminary," www.learn.jtsa.edu/topics/quote/archives/index.shtml, accessed October 28, 2005.

18. Chuck Swindoll, *Living on the Ragged Edge* (Waco: Word, 1985), 142.

19. Diane Butler-Bass, *Strength for the Journey* (New York: John Wiley and Sons, 2002), 43.

20. Robert Hooker, 1554–1600.

21. Copyright 1929, 1940, by Lesbia Scott (1898–1986).

22. "Immortal, invisible, God only wise, in light inaccessible hid from our eyes, most blessed, most glorious, the Ancient of Days, Almighty, victorious, Thy great Name we praise." Words: Walter C. Smith, *Hymns of Christ and the Christian Life,* 1876. Taken from 1 Timothy 1:17.

23. "Most people believe that physicists are explaining the world. Some physicists even believe that, but the Wu Li Masters know that they are only dancing with it." Gary Zukav, *The Dancing Wu Li Masters,* reissue edition (New York: Bantam, September 1, 1984), 8. The Chinese word for physics is *Wu Li,* "patterns of organic energy."

24. Reinhold Niebuhr, *Beyond Tragedy* (New York: Scribner, 1937), 4.

25. Charles Spurgeon, *Morning and Evening* (Peabody, MS: Hendrickson Publishers, 1991), 155.

26. Frederica Mathewes-Greene, "The Kissing Part," article from St. Paul's Greek Orthodox Church website, www.stpaulsirvine.org/html/kissingpart.html, July 2004.

27. www.adventureliving.com/home/wwr/index.html.

28. George Matheson, "O Love That Wilt Not Let Me Go," Church of Scotland magazine *Life and Work* (January 1882).

29. John Stackhouse, "God's Alchemy of Grace," *Faith Today* (May/June 2003).

30. T. S. Eliot, "Gerontian," *Collected Poems* (New York: Harcourt Brace, 1934), 5.

31. William Blake, "The Tyger," *Songs of Innocence and of Experience* (1794).

32. Kopp, *I Went to the Animal Fair,* 97.